Paranormal Phenomena

Look for these and other books in the Lucent Overview Series:

Paranormal Phenomena

by Patricia D. Netzley

Lucent
Books

LUCENT *Overview Series*

Library of Congress Cataloging-in-Publication Data

Netzley, Patricia D.
   Paranormal phenomena / by Patricia D. Netzley.
      p.   cm. — (Lucent overview series)
   Includes bibliographical references and index.
   Summary: Discusses paranormal phenomena including psychic
connections, predicting the future, the mind/body connection,
spirits, sprites, aliens, and faith healing.
   ISBN 1-56006-622-9 (lib. : alk. paper)
   1. Parapsychology—Juvenile literature.   [1. Parapsychology.]
   I. Title.   II. Series.
BF1031 .N48 2000
133—dc21
                                                      99-040473

Copyright © 2000 by Lucent Books, Inc.
P.O. Box 289011, San Diego, CA 92198-9011
Printed in the U.S.A.

Contents

Introduction

PARANORMAL PHENOMENA ARE creatures or occurrences that cannot be explained scientifically. Sightings of unidentified flying objects (UFOs), reports of alien abductions, mental telepathy, ghosts, and miracles all fall into this category.

Some people say that such phenomena are real, whether or not science can explain them. Others argue that if something is unexplainable by science, it must not be real. These two sides—believers and skeptics—engage in heated debates over whether reports of paranormal experiences are the product of hallucinations or something more substantial.

Meanwhile, researchers into paranormal phenomena continue to seek explanations. As Jerome Clark says in his book *Unexplained!*, "The three hardest words for human beings to utter are *I don't know.* We demand an accounting for every claim or experience, and when no accounting is available, someone will invent one for us."[1] Consequently scientists and psychologists have come up with a variety of theories for why paranormal phenomena exist, if they exist, but each new theory only fuels the arguments between believers and skeptics.

Clark takes a balanced view of these discussions, acknowledging that both sides of the debate have valid positions:

> Witnesses [to paranormal phenomena] often say, "I wouldn't have believed it if I hadn't seen it myself"—a statement that resonates with meaning. There are some things people believe

in not because they are ignorant, credulous, or crazy but because either they or persons they trust see them. Seeing is believing, indeed. . . .

There is, on the other hand, much to be said for skepticism. Skepticism need not be synonymous with . . . emotional crusades against heretical beliefs and unacceptable experiences. But a rational, balanced skepticism, one that is neither apologetic about its demand for persuasive evidence nor afraid to admit the limits of current knowledge, is to be preferred to mindless credulity. And where extraordinary claims are concerned, there is a great deal to be skeptical about.[2]

Whether scientists will ever solve the mysteries associated with paranormal phenomena remains to be seen. But to some people, having a solution is unimportant. According to polls conducted by major news organizations, more than half of all Americans currently believe in ghosts, reincarnation, and angels, although no scientific proof for any of these phenomena exists. Approximately 19 million people claim they have seen a UFO, although Clark argues:

A depiction of an unidentified flying object (UFO) passing over a highway.

To say that you have "seen" one is not necessarily to say that the anomaly lives on in the world when it is not briefly occupying your vision and scaring the daylights out of you. We may experience unbelievable things, but our experiences of them may tell us nothing about them except that they can be experienced. You can "see" a mermaid or a werewolf, but however impressive the experience may be to you, the rest of us cannot infer from that that mermaids and werewolves are "real."[3]

The definition of "real" is central to discussions of paranormal phenomena. What makes something real? What is reality? Is the world we are currently experiencing the only world in existence? Some people believe that ghosts and aliens inhabit another realm—the imaginal realm—with which some human minds can communicate. Other people believe that the "other realm" is actually heaven, or the afterlife, a place where spirits go after the physical body has died. Skeptics say that any vision of a strange being, even if others share that vision, is a hallucination. All of these theories are based on the concept that the mind is more complicated than science can currently explain—or may ever be able to explain.

A depiction of ghosts outside an old Western building.

1

Psychic Connections

PSYCHIC ABILITY HAS been the subject of more scientific studies than any other type of paranormal phenomena. The word *psychic* comes from the Greek *psyche,* which means *mind,* and refers to information received by the mind without the aid of the recognized senses (sight, hearing, taste, touch, and smell). Some people suggest that an unrecognized sense must be involved in this apparent mental transmission of information. Hence psychic abilities are often referred to as extrasensory perception, or ESP.

The most commonly reported type of ESP is telepathy, which is the direct communication of a thought or image from one human mind to another in real time. The second most common is clairvoyance, which occurs when the mind receives an extrasensory image of a place, object, or event without the involvement of a human "transmitter."

Early frauds

Telepathy and clairvoyance were the focus of the earliest research conducted by the Society for Psychical Research (SPR). This group was the first organization devoted to the investigation of paranormal activities, and it permanently changed the nature of such research. Prior to its founding in London in 1882, investigations into the paranormal were conducted by hobbyists under highly unscientific conditions. In contrast, SPR research was conducted using rigid methodology, and the group established a scholarly journal to share its procedures with the scientific community so that experiments could be repeated and results verified.

Nonetheless, several frauds were perpetrated against the SPR in its early years. For example, members of the SPR were fooled by four sisters who claimed they could communicate telepathically. During an SPR test, one of the young women was sent out of the room and the others were told a name or a number or shown a playing card or other object. They were then told to concentrate on what they had seen, and when the missing girl returned she was asked to reveal what her sisters were thinking. Although the girls failed to identify some of the objects, they got most of them right, and were particularly gifted at transmitting information about playing cards. The SPR accepted this as proof that their telepathy, then called thought-reading, was a valid mental skill.

However, in 1888 one member of the committee, Edmund Gurney, witnessed another demonstration of the sis-

Twins participate in extrasensory perception (ESP) tests.

ters' powers and realized that they had to be signaling to one another. The girls always fidgeted during their demonstrations, and Gurney theorized that their intricate body movements and loud sighs were actually an elaborate code. Without revealing his suspicion, he and several associates worked on translating the code, and eventually they were able to interpret the girls' messages. For example, the researchers discovered that an eye movement in a particular direction told the suit of a playing card. When Gurney confronted the girls with what he had learned, they confessed to the deceit.

Although many people subsequently criticized the SPR for not blindfolding the girls during their tests to make sure they could not cheat, another early fraud perpetrated against the SPR succeeded despite just such a precaution. In 1882 journalist Douglas Blackburn and hypnotist George Albert Smith claimed to have a telepathic connection with one another. To prove their claim in front of SPR investigators, a seated Smith was blindfolded and his ears were plugged. He was then covered with two thick blankets so that he sat in complete darkness. His chair rested on a rug heavy enough to muffle floor vibrations. Across the room, Blackburn was given an unfamiliar, nonsensical sketch to study, which Smith would then draw while under his blankets. Based on Blackburn's "telepathic" messages, Smith was able to reproduce the sketches with great accuracy, and SPR pronounced the men's psychic connection authentic.

Over twenty years later, Blackburn confessed that Smith's telepathy had been staged and explained how. While studying a sketch during the test, Blackburn had been allowed to draw it himself several times, and he would secretly place one of his drawings inside a tube encasing his pencil. When Smith "accidentally" dropped his own pencil, Blackburn would pass the pencil with the hidden drawing under Smith's blanket. Smith would then peek from beneath his blindfold and, using a hidden luminous slate that afforded him enough light to see, he would copy Blackburn's sketch perfectly in his own hand.

Because of Blackburn's confession—which was denied by Smith—and several previous incidents of inaccurate SPR authentication, for many years the public distrusted the research produced by the organization. At the same time, SPR began to take greater precautions while conducting its investigations and insisted on repeating its tests several times with different examiners.

As a result, the SPR now approaches its subjects much more methodically and skeptically than it did in its early years. Paul Chambers discusses this aspect of the Smith-Blackburn legacy in his book *Paranormal People:*

> [The fraud was] the result of bad scientific conditions, but then it must be remembered that Blackburn and Smith were some of the first people claiming psychic powers ever to be tested by scientists. It is easy with the aid of hindsight to criticize, but at the time parapsychology was in its absolute infancy. . . . These days the science . . . bases its work on the collection of volumes of information by performing repeated experiments on ordinary people under laboratory conditions.[4]

Standardized testing

Today the SPR and other organizations conduct research into ESP using a variety of standardized testing techniques. One of the first such tests was developed by the Institute of Parapsychology, a private organization that began as the Duke University Parapsychology Laboratory in 1930. Under the direction of its founder, Dr. Joseph Banks Rhine, the facility developed a pack of twenty-five cards, each with one of five different symbols: a star, a circle, a square, a cross, and a set of wavy lines. The person evaluating a subject's telepathic abilities selects one of the cards at random and, without showing the card to the subject, asks the subject to name the image on the card. This process is repeated for the full pack of cards.

Each test subject has a one-in-five chance of merely guessing the correct answer; a level of success much higher than this is considered an indication of psychic ability. In early tests with the cards, no respondent demonstrated a rate beyond chance. Then, in 1931, a student at Duke University, A. J. Linzmayer, provided 404 correct answers out of 1,500 tries; only 300 correct answers would have been expected by chance. In an additional 2,000 tests, Linzmayer continued to have a success rate that was higher than chance would allow.

Also in 1931, a Rhine associate named J. Gaither Pratt discovered another student he believed had psychic powers. Hubert Pearce, who was studying theology, attained better and more consistent scores on his tests than Linzmayer had. Pearce was tested for clairvoyance as well as telepathy; sometimes his tester looked at the card while asking him to name it, while other times the card was not viewed by the tester, also called the agent, until *after* Pearce named it. Some of the tests even took place with the agent and subject in different buildings.

Dr. J. B. Rhine, a parapsychologist at Duke University.

The Pratt-Pearce tests are among the most famous in psychic research, although Rhine soon discovered five more students who displayed a high accuracy rate with his cards. Dr. Richard S. Broughton, director of research at the Institute of Parapsychology and author of *Parapsychology: The Controversial Science,* reports that in a test conducted with Pratt in one building and Pearce in another, Pearce averaged 9.9 "hits," or successes, for every 25 cards tested, where chance predicts only 5 hits.

> Ultimately four separate experiments were done with a total of 558 hits out of 1,850 trials (where 370 would be expected by chance). The odds against chance for the series were literally astronomical, 22 billion-to-one.[5]

Disbelief and accusations

But despite such results, after Rhine published his work in scholarly journals and the articles were reprinted in popular magazines, he was attacked by other scientists. These attacks continued even after researchers at other scientific institutions were able to duplicate his results. Some people accused Rhine of sloppy methodology, while others insisted that Pearce had somehow cheated during the test, although they had no proof.

Criticism of psychic research also appeared in popular literature. For example, in his 1979 book *ESP, Seers, and Psychics: What the Occult* Really *Is,* magician and skeptic Milbourne Christopher put forth several theories on how Pearce might have duped Pratt, most involving Pearce finding some way to peek at Pratt's cards. Christopher also argued that mere coincidence could account for Pearce's successful test results. To illustrate his point, he gave the following example of a documented incident that seemed to be impossible by the rules of chance, but occurred nonetheless:

> An Associated Press story in the February 27, 1970, issue of the *New York Post* . . . [reports that] Mrs. Jack Greenway, while playing bridge at the Cocoa-Rockledge Country Club in Cocoa, Florida, dealt herself thirteen spades. Mrs. James Purgason received thirteen diamonds; Mrs. R. B. Deaton, thirteen hearts; and Mrs. Myron Stevens, thirteen clubs. The *Post* article continues: "*The Guinness Book of World Records* says: 'If all the people in the world were grouped in bridge fours and each four were dealt 120 hands per day, it would require 1,000,000,000,000 years before one "perfect" deal could be expected to recur.'"[6]

But despite criticisms like Christopher's, the public's belief in psychic ability soared. During the 1970s, when criticism was at its peak, surveys indicated that over 75 percent of the public supported the likelihood that telepathy and clairvoyance were valid mental skills. Today that figure remains high, largely because most people know someone who has experienced, or have themselves experienced, what seems to be an incident of telepathy in their daily lives. Dr. Rhine's Institute of Parapsychology also reported on this type of telepathy—that is, telepathy that took place not in a laboratory or as part of a test or demonstration, but as a unique event in the normal course of life. Dr. Rhine's wife and research partner, Louisa E. Rhine, was the first to realize the importance of such events.

Hunches and hallucinations

After information about the institute's research was reported in the media, the Rhines began receiving unsolicited letters that detailed the ESP experiences of ordinary people. Louisa started collecting these letters and studying them to determine patterns and categories of psychic events.

Approximately 30 percent of Louisa Rhine's letter-writers reported having a telepathic or clairvoyant experience that came in the form of a simple hunch, or an intuitive insight not based on any type of logic or inference. People reported just "knowing" what someone was thinking or that an event was happening or about to happen. One woman suddenly realized that her father was taking wedding vows while away on his vacation, even though she had no idea he was planning to get married at all.

Approximately 10 percent of the ESP experiences reported to Rhine were not hunches but hallucinated visions, sounds, or feelings that occurred during a fully awake state. For example, a woman reported that a vision of her

A man attempts to divulge the contents of an envelope using telepathy.

husband appeared in front of her at a time when he was several thousand miles away. Later she learned that at the time of her vision, her husband had been extremely sick and praying that he could be home with her. Another woman described an incident of a hallucinated pain:

> On November 8, 1961, shortly after I had arrived at the school where I teach, I went into the office. Suddenly an extremely severe pain struck my shoulder and chest, so intense that it made me cry out. The principal and other teachers who were in the office were alarmed. However, the intensity of the pain did not last, and I went on with my work.

> About an hour after this, my principal came to my room to tell me that I had a long-distance call. My aunt had suffered a heart attack as she and my mother were going downstairs. She had died instantly, with only my mother there. As well as we could estimate, it had happened about the time the severe pain had struck me.[7]

Dreams and ESP

The largest number of telepathic and clairvoyant messages reported to Louisa Rhine—approximately 60 percent—were received not in a waking state but during dreams. Many people dreamed of an accident or death only to find out later that their dream had been correct. For example, a grandmother wrote that she had awakened during the night after dreaming that her grandson was smothering in his crib blankets. When the grandmother called her daughter's home to ask that someone check on the baby, her son-in-law reported that he had already done so, and that the baby had indeed been smothering.

This apparent link between ESP and dreaming has led many investigators to examine the dream process and develop ways to test ESP in sleeping subjects. The earliest such tests were conducted in the 1970s at the Maimonides Community Mental Health Center in Brooklyn, New York. Researchers there concentrated on an image in a painting and tried to transmit it to a sleeping test subject. The sleeper's eyelids were monitored for rapid eye movements (REMs), which indicate when someone is dreaming, so that researchers would know when to awaken them.

Many investigators feel that a connection exists between ESP and the act of dreaming.

When awakened in the middle of a dream, people are far more likely to remember dream content, and the Maimonides test subjects were no exception. They were able to describe their dreams in detail, and these descriptions were then analyzed by a panel of judges who did not know which artwork had been used in the test. The judges matched dreams to paintings, and for certain test subjects their rate of success was high. One subject apparently dreamed of the correct image thirteen out of fifteen times.

Investigators into psychic phenomena have several theories for why the dreaming state might be conducive to

ESP. One theory is that the unconscious mind is more receptive to psychic connections because it is not distracted by sensory input. To test this theory, researchers developed another way to isolate the mind from the senses. The ESP-ganzfeld experiment (after the German word *ganzfeld,* which means "entire field," or total environment) relies on depriving the senses of stimulation, much as occurs during sleep.

The test subject is placed in a special soundproof room that is temperature- and pressure-controlled for maximum comfort. The subject also wears headphones that supply crackling white noise, which prevents the subject from hearing any one specific sound. Special eye covers and lightbulbs are used to make the subject's eyes see a diffused light rather than a specific image.

As with the dream experiments, ganzfeld tests involve attempts to identify pictures. While the test subject relaxes in the first room, the experimenter sits in a second room randomly choosing slides or videotapes that are then projected into a third room, where a "sender" views them and tries to mentally transmit them to the subject. Some of these experiments have had an impressive success rate, but skeptics offer a variety of reasons for this, including luck, fraud, and faulty research procedures. Nonetheless, both supporters and critics have suggested that further studies are needed to determine why the success rate might be so high.

Viewing distant places

More research has also been called for regarding "remote viewing," a form of clairvoyance in which people can describe places and objects from a distance. In remote-viewing experiments, the "sender" visits a site while the "receiver" sits in a room and tries to sketch what the sender is seeing. On occasion, remote viewers have been able to provide reliable though crude information about terrain, buildings, and other objects at the remote-viewing site. Once again, some skeptics have suggested that fraud might be involved with these successes. Various methods of cheating have been suggested, including the possibility that the remote viewer was tipped off in advance regarding which site would be used in the experiment.

However, U.S. government investigations into remote viewing, which took place from the early 1970s until 1995, were conducted in such a way as to eliminate the possibility of cheating, and in some cases the results achieved were far better than chance would allow. But critics maintain that the methodology of the tests was flawed, even though the flaws are not yet apparent. Ray Hyman, a skeptic asked by the government to evaluate the tests, explains that

> A hit rate better than the chance baseline of 20 percent can be considered evidence for remote viewing, of course, only if all other nonpsychic possibilities have been eliminated. . . . The elimination of these sources of above-chance hitting is not an easy task. The history of psychical research and parapsychology presents example after example of experiments that were advertised as having eliminated all nonpsychic possibilities and that were discovered by subsequent investigators to have had subtle and unsuspected biases. Often it takes years before the difficulties with a new experimental design or program come to light.[8]

Psychic sleuths

A variation of remote viewing is the clairvoyance used to identify the whereabouts of a missing person or murder suspect. This type of psychic ability has been reported for hundreds of years. For example, in his 1693 book *Occult Physics or a Treatise on the Divining Rod,* Pierre Le Lorrain mentions a French peasant named Jacques Aymar who tracked down a murderer using a divining rod, a stick that supposedly points the way to desired objects if used by a psychic. The murderer he identified soon confessed to the crime, but subsequent tests on Aymar's abilities produced mixed results. Sometimes he was able to identify the perpetrators of mock crimes, but other times he failed miserably.

A more reliable psychic detective was Florence Sternfels, who worked with police and military officials to solve dozens of cases during the 1960s. Arthur Lyons and Marcello Truzzi describe her successes in their book *The Blue*

Sense: Psychic Detectives and Crime, which traces the history of psychic sleuthing and its impact on modern policework. They report that there was ample evidence regarding Sternfels's successes:

> During World War II Sternfels was involved with two military cases. On one occasion, she reportedly told authorities . . . that a worker with dynamite in his dinner pail was planning sabotage. They searched and found a worker who fit the bill. Another incident from this period was related to a report by Colonel (then Major) Arthur Burks. Dolly Miller, the seven-year-old daughter of a marine officer . . . was kidnapped and brutally murdered. When Dolly was reported missing, they searched for her for weeks without success. Then Burks contacted Florence. She told him Dolly was dead and correctly described a place in a swamp where they could find her. After they found Dolly's body but came up with no clues as to who did it, Burks again contacted Florence. She then fully described the murder and named Dolly's killer as being Joe Keller. Keller was a civilian, not a marine, and he had been conspicuously and seemingly earnestly involved in the earlier search for Dolly. When Keller was confronted with Florence's detailed description, he confessed. He was tried and sentenced to life imprisonment.[9]

Some believe that, in the hands of a psychic, a divining rod can point the way to a desired person or object.

Modern psychic detectives also exhibit varying degrees of success. Many have provided information that turns out to be either inaccurate or too general. A few, however, have been correct about specific aspects of a crime. Lyons and Truzzi describe a case in which psychic Greta Alexander helped Detective William Fitzgerald of Alton, Illinois, find a body during the early 1980s:

> Alexander . . . circled an area where the police should conduct their search. The area had been gone over many times before, so the investigators were pessimistic about turning up anything, but decided to give it one more try. This time, searchers found the woman's skeletal remains. . . . [According to Fitzgerald, there were] twenty-two "hits" Alexander had made concerning the finding of the body. Among them: the head and a foot would be separated from the body, that the letter *S* would be important in the discovery, and that the man who found the remains would have a "bad hand." The skull was found five feet from the body, the left foot was missing, and the auxiliary policeman who found the body, Steve Trew, had a deformed left hand, the result of an accident. "I was skeptical to begin with," Fitzgerald told the press, "but I guess I'm going to have to be a believer now."[10]

Lyons and Truzzi also report on skeptics' reactions to such events, who argue that "the predictions and clairvoyant visions of the psychics in virtually all of the cases are vague and self-fulfilling, often odds-on guesses, the significance of which is only colored in later by gullible cops, ESP advocates, and a public that wants to believe."[11] And in fact many police officers remain unconvinced that psychics are valuable assets to them, believing that the psychics' tips waste time more often than they provide answers. For this reason, some researchers have suggested that a database be created to track the accuracy of psychics when locating missing persons and providing crime details. Meanwhile, skeptics continue to point out that despite years of research into telepathy and clairvoyance, no study has yet proven that these phenomena are real.

2

Predicting the Future: Psychic Ability or Gullibility?

RESEARCH INTO PSYCHIC ability has primarily focused on testing telepathic or clairvoyant messages sent in real time. However, according to Dr. Richard Broughton, a leading investigator into psychic phenomena, more than half of all psychic experiences impart information about events that have not yet occurred. These experiences fall into three categories: premonitions, precognitions, and predictions.

Premonitions are vague feelings that occur while a person is awake. An example of this would be the feeling that a friend's plane is about to crash or that a relative is about to call. In contrast, precognitions are specific images of future events. They often occur during dreams or meditative states. Dr. Broughton describes one woman's experience with precognition in his book *Parapsychology: The Controversial Science:*

> [She] had a vivid dream in which her husband was out hunting and had been accidentally shot and killed by his hunting partner. It had been an unusually vivid dream—unlike her normal dreams—and she had awakened from it in a cold sweat. Her husband did go hunting occasionally and she debated whether or not she should tell him the dream. Since he had no immediate plans to go hunting and he had already announced that his schedule would not permit him to do so that season, the woman decided not to mention the dream. About two weeks later her husband was unexpectedly

invited to go hunting, and equally unexpectedly he found the time to do so. Again the woman debated whether or not to tell him about the dream, but this time she feared that perhaps the act of telling him might somehow bring the event to pass, and she knew in any case that her husband would ridicule her concern over "just a dream." . . . The next morning her husband did go hunting, and in a freak accident almost exactly like the one the woman had seen in her dream, his partner accidentally shot and killed him.[12]

Predictions are different from premonitions and precognitions in that they are the result of deliberate attempts to foretell the future. They often involve the use of divining tools such as crystal balls, tarot cards, tea leaves, lines in the palm of the hand, and astrological charts. In some cases, no such tools are involved; the person making the prediction claims to have received a vision from a Supreme Being or other spiritual being. In such cases, the prediction is called a prophecy.

Studies into premonitions

While conducting scientific studies into premonition and precognition, researchers identified certain traits shared by those who experience the phenomena. In his book *Paranormal People,* Paul Chambers describes the common characteristics:

Those who have studied [these phenomena] have noticed that the people most liable to experience precognition are women in their mid-forties and that 85 percent of their premonitions involve death or disaster. Other studies have noted, perhaps unkindly, that many of these people are also neurotic and have an inflated idea of their success rates. One particularly interesting study by C. Tart in 1993 found that 32 percent of marijuana users reported precognitive experiences and that they were also liable to score higher in laboratory

A fortune teller peers into her crystal ball.

tests. In fact, attempts to study precognition in the laboratory have so far had a low success rate. Skeptics use this as evidence of its non-existence; others point out that its spontaneous nature makes it difficult to know when it will occur next.[13]

Changing the future

Part of the controversy over whether or not precognition is even possible revolves around the nature of time. Various theories have been advanced regarding how time progresses, and some people have suggested that the past, present, and future all exist simultaneously. Under this theory, psychics are receiving images of events that are actually taking place, much as with remote viewing, rather than of events that have yet to occur. Those who support this view disagree on whether such a system eliminates the possibility that the future can be changed.

In the 1930s, parapsychologist Louisa Rhine studied 191 precognitive experiences involving subsequent attempts to change the future. In 60, or 31 percent, of the cases, the person who experienced the precognitive dream was unable to stop a predicted event from happening, often because of incomplete information. In 131, or 69 percent, the person who experienced the phenomenon, also called the experient, was successful in stopping the event, typically because the precognitive dream was rich in detail.

One example of someone who was unable to stop a predicted event was a woman who dreamed of a fiery plane crash at the shore of a nearby lake. Although she told friends about her dream, she did not contact any authorities because she did not know the airline or the time the event would occur. A few days later she saw a particular plane flying overhead and recognized it as the plane in her dream. She told her husband to alert the fire department so that their personnel would be on hand to douse the flames, but by then it was too late. The crash had already occurred.

A streetcar conductor who dreamed of a fatal crash involving his streetcar and a truck was actually able to prevent the crash. In his dream, he clearly saw the precise route of the streetcar as well as a vivid picture of the truck and its occupants. While at work the next day, he recognized a series of events from his dream, and he realized that the crash was about to occur. He suddenly stopped his streetcar—barely in time to miss hitting a truck that matched the one he had envisioned.

Such stories suggest that the future can be changed. However, Dr. Broughton reports that the researchers at his parapsychology institute have heard many stories of people who try to stop a precognitive dream from coming true only to inadvertently cause the very disaster they were trying to prevent.

Broughton also reports that studies of precognitive dreams must take into account the dreams' unreliability:

> Often an individual's recollection of the psychic experience becomes more and more like the confirming event as time goes on. Just as a tale grows in the telling, the recollection of the experience—which itself may have been vague in the first place, especially if it was a dream or an impression—may come to "fit" reality far more closely than it did originally. A dream of an auto accident may grow to seem more precognitive as details of the real event become intermingled with recollections of the dream.[14]

In many of Rhine's cases, the person who experienced the precognitive dream told others about it before the predicted event took place. Nonetheless, Broughton says that these reports might still have been subject to human error because "the dramatic or frightening nature of the psychic experience might cause a person to misperceive the details of a complicated event in such a way that they appear to 'confirm' the psychic experience."[15] In other words, because of the heightened emotions surrounding the situation, not only the experient but also those who heard his or her prediction might be mistaken about the prediction's degree of accuracy.

Prophets

Debates over accuracy also surround the third type of prediction, the prophecy. Many of the earliest prophecies are related to religious beliefs. The faithful accept them as valid; others do not. For example, Christians believe that the Old Testament of the Bible foretold the life of Jesus Christ, which is described in the New Testament. Skeptics suggest that the authors of the New Testament wrote about Jesus' life specifically with the Old Testament prophecies in mind, altering their story to make it appear as though the prophecies had been fulfilled.

Dr. Broughton believes that unless a prophecy is connected to one's religious faith, it will typically be greeted with skepticism because in modern times "precognitive experiences are among the most difficult to accept at face value. People are willing to allow that there might be unknown means of communicating information between people contemporaneously, but to foresee a future event—that is just too much to swallow."[16]

A painting depicts Jesus Christ healing the sick and diseased.

In earlier times, secular prophets were considered valuable to society. One such prophet was Robert Nixon, a simple-minded fifteenth-century English plow boy whose prophecies were well documented. In 1467, Nixon suddenly exclaimed in front of several witnesses, "Now Dick! Now Harry! Oh, ill done, Dick! Oh, well done, Harry! Harry has gained the day!"[17] The next morning, the witnesses learned that this exclamation coincided with the death of King Richard III in battle at the hands of Henry VII. Since the English nicknames for Richard and Henry are Dick and Harry, this news caused much amazement, and word of Nixon's telepathy soon reached the newly crowned King Henry VII.

England's King Henry VII believed it possible to predict the future.

The king ordered Nixon brought to court for verification of his powers and learned that the boy was able to predict the future. Nixon's predictions were carefully recorded by royal scribes, and after several of these predictions came true, Nixon was considered a valued aide to the king. However, this caused some jealousy among others at court, and King Henry ordered one of his officers to protect the boy. While Henry feared Nixon would be murdered, Nixon predicted a different fate for himself: starvation. Those who knew him thought this foolish—until the officer protecting Nixon locked him in a secret room and, having been called away unexpectedly, forgot about him. Nixon did indeed starve to death before he was found.

Nostradamus

Perhaps the best-known secular prophet is Michel de Nostredame, or Nostradamus, a Frenchman who lived from 1503 to 1566. His first predictions were weather-related, but beginning in 1555 he published a series of four-line verses, called quatrains, that prophesied major events. The quatrains were symbolic in nature and as such could be interpreted in more than one way; consequently skeptics argue that claims of their accuracy are highly subjective.

Nonetheless, one of Nostradamus's first predictions, published in 1555, made him famous in his own time.

A four-hundred-year-old woodcut depicts the infamous prophet, Nostradamus.

The young lion will overcome the older one, in a field of combat in a single fight: He will pierce his eyes in their golden cage; two wounds in one, then he dies a cruel death.[18]

Four years after this quatrain appeared, King Henry II of France was killed during a jousting tournament when a staff pierced his face helmet. On his shield was his emblem, a lion, and he did indeed die a cruel death, because it took him several days to die.

Nostradamus also predicted things that seemed to come true after his lifetime. Of these, perhaps the best known are the following quatrains, which many believe deal with the rise of Adolf Hitler:

The life and actions of a man resembling German dictator Adolf Hitler were prophesied by Nostradamus in the late 1500s.

Liberty shall not be recovered, a black, fierce, villainous, evil man shall occupy it, when the ties of his alliance are wrought. Venice shall be vexed by Hister.

Beasts wild with hunger will cross the rivers, the greater part of the battlefield will be against Hister. He will drag the leader in a cage of iron, when the child of Germany observes no law.[19]

Although interpretations of the quatrains vary, most people who believe in Nostradamus's predictions say that Hister is Hitler, the German dictator who took away liberty, formed alliances, and annexed Venice, Italy, during his rise to power. His soldiers crossed many rivers, and his iron submarines blockaded, or caged, Great Britain, which was then considered the leader among European nations.

Skeptics point out that translators of the original verses, which appeared in a dialect called Languedoc, have in many cases selected words that have a bearing on the predictions' accuracy. In his book *Paranormal People,* Paul Chambers examines a quatrain that many people believe predicted the Great London Fire of 1666.

Many feel that the Great Fire of London in 1666 was predicted by Nostradamus more than a century earlier.

The blood of the good shall be wanting in London,
Burnt by the fire of twenty and three the sixes,
The old lady shall fall from her high place,
Of the same sect many shall be killed.[20]

Chambers explains that "three the sixes" might refer to the year 1666, and "the old lady" was a nickname for St. Paul's Cathedral, which was destroyed in the fire. However, he adds that "the old lady" can also be translated as "the eccentric woman" and the word "fire" can also be translated as "thunderbolt." He points out that at the time the quatrain appeared, many of Nostradamus's contemporaries believed it referred to the then-prevalent persecution by Catholics of those in the Protestant religion. Chambers concedes that prophecies like Nostradamus's cannot be taken as proof that ESP exists, because "much twisting and turning goes on to make historical events fit the prophecies that some people have attributed to them."[21]

At the same time, Chambers argues that some prophets do seem to have some kind of psychic gift. He specifically mentions Kenneth Odhar, a prophet who lived in Scotland during the seventeenth century. Odhar's predictions, which were written down by a friend, are harder to dismiss because they were extremely specific. On one occasion he stopped at a particular spot and said it would be the site of a great battle involving a Scottish clan. Nearly a century later, in 1748, a battle fitting that description did indeed take place. Similarly, Odhar predicted that a certain village would be destroyed by a flood. Since there was no large body of water near the village, Odhar's contemporaries thought this prediction silly. But years later a dam was built to create an artificial lake nearby, and in 1966 the dam overflowed and flooded the village. Skeptics consider this a coincidence.

Astrological forecasts

For obvious reasons, the accuracy of prophets who make such long-term predictions cannot be validated during their lifetimes. However, researchers have attempted to determine the accuracy of people making short-term predictions such as those made using astrological forecasts.

Astrology is an ancient belief that a person's character and future are determined, or at least influenced, by the position of the sun, the moon, the planets, and the stars at the time of his or her birth. Various measurements of celestial bodies are used to create a horoscope, which is a description of what will happen during a given time period in a person's life. The daily horoscope that appears in newspapers is based on only one of these measurements; therefore many astrologers insist that such horoscopes do not offer a true idea of how accurate their forecasts can be. In addition, more detailed horoscopes offer information not only about future events but also about a person's character traits.

Researchers who examined the most thorough astrological forecasts found no evidence that they accurately predict events or identify character traits. Most forecasts provide general information that is subject to interpretation, as skeptic George Abell explains:

> Most people who have their horoscopes analyzed by an astrologer say that the descriptions they receive of themselves are accurate. However, the descriptions are generally vague and sometimes contradictory, and they almost always reveal a good grasp of human psychology on the part of the analyzer.[22]

Several experiments have been designed to prove that some people are eager to believe a horoscope suits them perfectly, even when it does not. For example, for an ABC-News special entitled "The Power of Belief," reporter John Stossel had an astrologer create a detailed horoscope of a mass murderer. He then gathered together a group of people and gave each one of them an envelope, telling them that inside was a horoscope prepared specially for each individual. Unbeknownst to them, they had each been given the same horoscope, that of the mass murderer. Nonethe-

Horoscope charts utilize planet and star positions to predict the future.

less, after reading the detailed description of "their" character, most of the people said the horoscope accurately reflected their personality traits.

The nocebo effect

Stossel suggests that people are equally gullible about predictions of future events, interpreting them as correct because they want to believe in them and perhaps even making later choices that will cause the forecast to come true. He points out that doctors have long known that if a person believes he is sick, that person can actually make himself ill. This effect is called the nocebo effect. A companion effect, the placebo effect, has also been verified in countless studies in which people are given a sugar pill and told it is a particular type of medicine that will make them feel better. After taking the "medicine," test subjects do indeed report feeling better until they learn the truth.

To illustrate the nocebo effect, Stossel says that if a fortune-teller predicts you will soon have back pain, then "you'll notice every pain that you do have. Every morning you get up and you roll out of bed, if you get a twinge of any kind you'll say, 'Hey, there it is.' You start to feel bad immediately."[23] Similarly, if a psychic predicts that you will become romantically involved with a stranger the following year, you will probably be more receptive to meeting new people and might subconsciously cause the prediction to come true.

Unusual messengers

Nonetheless, people continue to seek out fortune-tellers and divination paraphernalia. One example of the latter is a tarot-card deck. During the period from 1974 to 1994, U.S. Games Systems, the largest distributor of tarot cards, sold approximately 15 million tarot decks. Interestingly, tarot cards were first used as early as the fifteenth century, not to predict the future but to play a card game.

All tarot decks have seventy-eight cards with pictures on them, although the pictures can vary from deck to deck. Tarot-card readers use these pictures to form interpretations about, or "read," the future. However, tarot reading is highly subjective, and some psychics admit that they use the cards only as meditation tools. In *Adventures of a Psychic,* a biography of modern psychic Sylvia Brown, author Antoinette May notes:

> In the early days, Sylvia charged five dollars and used tarot cards. People didn't always realize that the cards were merely a means of altering consciousness and achieving focus. At one session, Sylvia told a client that she had a throat problem. "Yes, you're right," the woman responded, "but where's the sore throat card?" Before long, Sylvia realized that she no longer needed the cards; she could confront her clients' problems head-on.[24]

Some believe that tarot cards can be used to help forsee the future.

Sylvia Brown claims not only to be a clairvoyant who can receive images about future events, but also a

channeler, or someone who receives predictions from the dead. Channelers claim that spirits take over their bodies and speak through them. In Brown's case, she claims that she can put herself in a trance, whereupon the spirit of an Aztec/ Incan woman named Iena, whom Brown nicknamed Francine, enters her body and answers questions posed by those seeking information about the past, present, and future, as well as about the spirit world.

James Randi and his Pigasus Award. The award is given annually to the person with the most outrageous paranormal claims.

One of the most famous channelers is J. Z. Knight, who claims that her body is often taken over by the spirit of Ramtha, a thirty-five-thousand-year-old warrior from the Lost City of Atlantis. Ramtha's predictions about the future are vague. Nonetheless, thousands of people pay hundreds of dollars to attend Knight's seminars. She currently has her own school, the Ramtha School of Enlightenment, which attracts three thousand students for each half-year session.

In the late 1980s, former magician and professional skeptic James Randi attempted to prove that supporters of people like Knight are misguided. Randi has debunked thousands of claims related to paranormal phenomena, and to discredit channelers he devised an elaborate hoax. He taught a young man named Jose Alvarez to act like a channeler and, through a variety of ruses, convinced the Australian media that Jose was a famous South American channeler whose body was often taken over by "Carlos," a two-thousand-year-old spirit from Venezuela. After the media reported on Jose's amazing ability, people flocked to his public appearances. They also accepted his intentionally meaningless advice and predictions as valuable, and offered to pay thousands of dollars for some crystals he claimed would heal vague aches and pains.

Even more surprising, after the hoax was revealed, many of these people continued to express belief in "Carlos." In an interview with John Stossel, Jose Alvarez said, "At the end, there were people saying, 'We know everything they're saying about you. We don't care. We believe in you.'"[25] James Randi added, "No amount of evidence, no matter how good it is or how much there is of it, is ever going to convince the true believer to the contrary."[26] Some believers, however, say the same thing about skeptics, suggesting that no amount of evidence will ever be enough to convince a skeptic that psychic phenomena are real.

3

Altered States: The Mind/Body Connection

SOME PARANORMAL PHENOMENA involve an altered state of consciousness, a condition where the mind is awake yet not in its normal state. Channeling, for example, begins with the channeler going into a trance, which is a waking mental condition that appears much like sleep.

Scientists disagree about whether or not altered states can exist without the use of drugs or the presence of mental illness. This disagreement applies even to hypnosis, which was once widely accepted as an altered state. Hypnosis is a seemingly trancelike condition that apparently enhances a person's memory, diminishes the sensation of pain, and leaves the mind open to suggestions made by the hypnotist. However, many scientists now consider it the result of normal brain functions. Reporter Roger Highfield discusses both sides of the issue:

> Most scientists now reject the traditional view of hypnosis as a special condition of the brain that is manifested in a sleeplike state, or trance. . . . Some theorists still see hypnosis as an "altered state" which can produce changes in perception and behaviour not capable of being induced by "normal" human processes. But others argue that the phenomena associated with hypnosis can be explained in terms of ordinary human psychological processes such as imagination and relaxation.[27]

Out-of-body experiences

More unusual forms of altered states have generated even greater controversy. For example, scientists heatedly debate whether out-of-body experiences (OBEs) are possible. An OBE is the feeling that one's mind has become separated from one's body. In approximately 80 percent of OBEs, the experient seems to be observing events from above his or her physical body, while during the remainder of OBEs, the experient seems to be far from the body. For example, some experients report seeing their own bodies lying in a hospital bed, while others report observing doctors and nurses elsewhere in the hospital. One OBE experient, Robert Munroe, reported a series of OBEs during which he would lie down to rest and suddenly find himself observing a variety of distant landscapes and events from high above the ground.

Studies suggest that approximately one-fourth of the population will experience an OBE at some point in time,

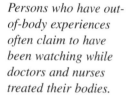

Persons who have out-of-body experiences often claim to have been watching while doctors and nurses treated their bodies.

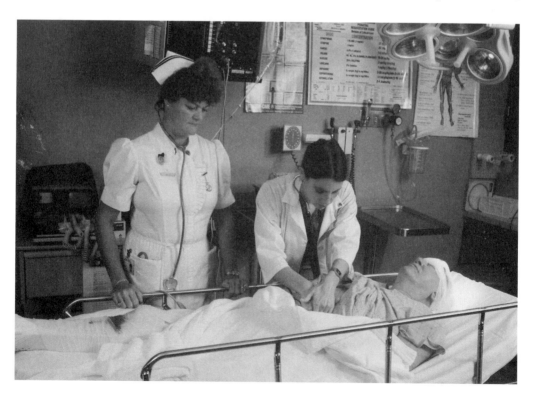

although typically only once in a lifetime. In a few cases like Munroe's, the OBE is preceded by relaxation, but in most cases the OBE is triggered by an accident, illness, or episode of severe pain, or by a drug- or anesthesia-induced state. In his book *Death and Consciousness,* David H. Lund cites the case of Ed Morrell, whose spirit would travel to distant places while he was being physically tortured in an Arizona prison. Lund says that many of the events Morrell observed were later confirmed, including a shipwreck the prisoner could not have known about.

Hallucinations

In studies of people who have experienced repeated OBEs, certain common traits have been discovered. First, these people have a strong ability to resist distraction. They also have a greater tendency to dream vividly, to practice meditation, and to fantasize, and they are highly susceptible to hypnosis.

Consequently, many psychologists and skeptics believe that OBEs represent a fantasy, a hallucination, or a product of simple imagination. James Alcock promotes this theory in his article "Psychology and Near-Death Experiences":

> Even in everyday memory processes there is a hint of this kind of phenomenon. Imagine yourself as you sat having dinner last evening. What do you "see"? Virtually everyone visualizes a vantage point outside the body. That memory, like most memories, is a construction, a partial invention. Again, think of yourself lying on the beach, and what do you "see"? Not the world around you as viewed through your own eyes, as you originally saw it, but in all likelihood you again see yourself as part of the scene.[28]

Some psychologists suggest that the out-of-body experience is an example of depersonalization, a sense of psychological detachment that often accompanies stress or trauma. People who have suffered physical abuse, for example, often report that they felt they were watching the event happen to someone else. However, such theories do not account for the fact that many OBEs begin with the experient in a state of relaxation or meditation. They also do not account for OBEs that include detailed descriptions of events the experient could not have physically observed.

Of course, in some cases, the experients' reports could have been fabricated or the result of exaggeration. But in many cases, there are witnesses who can verify the details of the experience. For example, in his book *Closer to the Light,* Dr. Melvin Morse describes the case of an eight-year-old boy named Jimmy who was able to describe things he saw while dead.

> Jimmy was fishing from a bridge when he slipped from his perch on the railing and hit his head on a rock in the water below. The doctor's report says that Jimmy had stopped breathing and was without a pulse when a police officer pulled him from the deep water in which he had floated facedown for at least five minutes. The policeman performed CPR for thirty minutes until the hospital helicopter arrived, but he reported that the boy was dead on the scene when they started the rush to the hospital.

> The boy lived. Two days later, he was out of his coma. "I know what happened when I fell off that bridge," he told his physician. . . . He proceeded to describe his entire rescue in vivid detail, including the name of the police officer who tried to resuscitate him, the length of time it took for the helicopter to arrive on the scene, and many of the lifesaving procedures used on him in the helicopter and at the hospital. He knew all of this, he said, because he had been observing from outside his body the whole time.[29]

Some psychologists suggest that such experiences can be explained by the brain's subconscious awareness of what is going on around it. Perhaps before Jimmy was truly dead, he heard various voices and sounds that led him to guess what was being done to him. Later, after he was revived, he merely filled in the details based on his knowledge of typical medical procedures and of the area where he fell.

But Dr. Richard Broughton points out that some OBEs cannot be explained this way:

> Collections of OBE cases reveal numerous instances in which the OBEer was able to describe accurately details of situations or events that were far too distant to be accounted for by sensory leakage. Sometimes the OBEer described specific events that took place while his or her body was incapacitated, which were not likely to have been inferred or anticipated. For exam-

" . . . And then I realized, IT WAS ME!! . . . I was floating over the whole fish bowl, I looked down and there was MY BODY!! . . . attached to me by a silver cord!! . . . There was an entire universe of wonderment and beauty, then a voice saying, 'GO BACK'!!"

ple, one man not only left his body on the operating table but, after watching the operation for a while, left the room and observed a particular interaction between a nurse and a doctor elsewhere in the hospital (which was later confirmed).[30]

Near-death experiences

As in Jimmy's case, many OBEs involve near-death experiences (NDEs), in which the experient has died and been brought back to life. But with many NDEs, the experient does not simply observe events going on in a hospital room. The mind apparently travels further, to the brink of what some people believe is the spiritual afterlife.

Dr. Melvin Morse offers a classic example of an NDE narrative involving a seventeen-year-old girl named Cindi who went into cardiac arrest while doing drugs.

> I passed out in my car. The next thing I remember was floating above my body and watching the doctors pushing on my chest. I now know that they were inside my chest, but I couldn't see that. All I could see was them working on me, and I couldn't really see any of the details.
>
> I then passed into a room filled with all of my friends. The room was very large and open at the top. It was like looking out at the sky. Sparks would fill the air and streaks of light zoomed up from the earth and burst into rainbows. I wanted very much to be one of those sparks, but I didn't know how to lift myself up and become one.
>
> I wanted to leave the room, but the door was closed. I knew if I opened it, I could never return. I was afraid of the door but wanted to go through it too, if you know what I mean.
>
> My dead grandfather then came to help me. He was a very religious man. He took me by the hand and said, "Go back to your body. You have work to do." Then he led me out of the room and back to my body. The next thing I remember, I was awake.[31]

Morse acknowledges that Cindi's experience could have been caused at least in part by things she heard going on during her resuscitation. He says, "When her family doctor whispered in her ear that the decision to return is up to her, could his voice somehow have become mixed up in her mind with that of her dead grandfather's? Possibly, but whoever was responsible, she responded well."[32]

However, the feeling of being apart from one's body, seeing lights or sparks, and visiting with dead relatives are all common aspects of NDEs. Although no two NDEs are the same, they do share certain features, and researchers have identified five basic stages of an NDE. These stages occur in order, which means that if a man is brought back to life during the third stage, he will not experience the fourth stage. Consequently there are far more NDEs involving the first stage than the fifth.

The first stage, which occurs as the person is dying, is a feeling of complete peace; the second stage, after death has occurred, is the feeling that the spirit has left the body; the third stage is the perception that the spirit is traveling through some dark place, usually a tunnel; the fourth stage is the perception that the spirit is approaching a place of light; and the fifth stage is the feeling that the spirit is entering the light, wherein experients find a place of great beauty. In rare cases, however, the experient ends up in a place later identified as "hell." For example, in his book *An Introduction to Parapsychology,* H. J. Irwin offers a narrative of one NDE in which a woman enters a building after arriving in the place of light. There she meets "the devil," who gives her a goblet of fire:

> I screamed, dropped the goblet and ran. I didn't know where I was running to and then I saw a big fence, a stone fence, and the gates opened and I passed through. Then I came to another fence made out of iron bars and that just opened and again I passed through. All the time I was getting warmer and warmer and brighter and brighter.[33]

A representation of the bright light common to NDE claims.

Many NDEs involve a review of the type of life a person lived. At some point during the third stage, approximately one in four experients see vivid images of what they did during their lives, which they typically view with detachment rather than anxiety. As part of this life review, they become aware that there is a decision to be made about whether or not they should go back into their bodies. Sometimes they feel as though an otherworldly being is there beside them, either making the decision or trying to help them make the decision for themselves, or they might see the spirit of a dead relative who becomes involved in the decision-making process. In any case, someone makes the decision, and the NDE ends with the person being resuscitated.

Dr. Broughton uses a composite narrative to illustrate this type of decision, as well as the stages of a typical NDE:

> I remember the pain, like my whole chest just seized up and I thought to myself, "This must be a heart attack." Then the pain just went away, and suddenly I felt so peaceful. Next thing I knew, I could see myself on the bed, as if I was looking down from the ceiling. The nurse came running in—must have been some noise I made—and she checked me. Then she grabbed the phone and said something like, "Call a code." I felt like I should tell her not to bother, I was just fine, but that seemed like too much effort. I was so peaceful. The nurse started working on my chest, but I sort of turned away. Suddenly I was outside in some beautiful garden, with sunlight and flowers. I walked—or sort of floated—down a path toward an entrance thing. When I started to go to her I heard a voice—or I think I heard a voice—telling me that it was not time yet, and that I had to go back. I didn't want to go back, but I couldn't say anything. Then things go gray, and the next thing I remember was that young doctor.[34]

Life after death

As with out-of-body experiences, some psychologists believe that near-death experiences are fantasies or hallucinations, possibly caused by the medications used during medical procedures, or the result of depersonalization. Many others support a slightly different view: The process of dying causes changes in the brain, and these changes create the near-death images. For example, research has

Most hallucinations include distorted views of reality, which some researchers believe are caused by a lack of oxygen to the brain.

shown that oxygen deprivation, which occurs during dying, can cause hallucinations as well as the feeling that the spirit is outside of the body. Changes in electrical activity within the brain can also trigger vivid images, and scientists suspect that certain chemicals released by the brain in times of stress might do so as well.

However, images caused by brain disturbances are random, whereas NDE images are always part of an orderly story and seem to describe an actual event. Therefore some scientists suggest that NDEs are actually memories of the birth experience. Under this theory, the tunnel in an NDE story represents the birth canal, the light at the end of it represents the lights of the delivery room, and the voices of dead relatives are reminiscent of the voices of those who were present in the delivery room.

But some researchers argue that this theory does not make sense given what is known about brain death, particularly in regard to the light at the end of the tunnel. Dr. Melvin Morse says that there is no "biochemical or psychological explanation for why we would experience a bright light as the final stage of bodily death":

The rigidly reductionistic among us could explain NDEs in the following manner: A person is faced with a life-threatening event. He or she leaves the physical body and watches what is happening in a detached and depersonalized manner. . . . As we know . . . this can sometimes be explained as the right temporal lobe [of the brain] being stimulated by a lack of oxygen.

Then there is a life review, seeing lights and people, hearing noises, having feelings of great joy and peace and seeing heavenly places. Surely, the skeptics say, these are simple psychological events that can be explained by examining the brain's organic processes.

As the brain begins its final dying process, there is a collapse of the visual fields and tunnel vision results. The eyes are no longer seeing, and the brain can no longer interpret what it sees. The tunnel becomes dark and the organism dies. . . . And then—there's light! Where does this light come from? The brain has nearly stopped functioning. The psychological processes I've just described took place in a few minutes . . . , and now all mental functions have ceased. One would assume that the bodily functions would simply cease, that there would be eternal darkness. Then why the light?[35]

Morse criticizes skeptics for not even considering the possibility that the spirit survives the death of the body and says that more research is needed before anyone can declare that this is not the case. He quotes Dr. Wilder Penfield, a top expert on the brain, who says, "It is obvious that science can make no statement at present in regard to the question of man's existence after death, although every thoughtful man must ask that question. Whether the mind is truly a separate element or whether, in some way not yet apparent, it is an expression of neuronal action, the decision must await . . . further scientific evidence."[36]

Reincarnation

An even more controversial paranormal phenomenon related to dying is reincarnation, the concept that the spirit not only survives death but is later given a new life in another body. A belief in reincarnation is part of some religions, including Hinduism, and throughout history there have been stories of children suddenly remembering details of past lives.

For example, in 1926 three-year-old Jagdish Chandra of India told his father and several witnesses that he was once a man named Jai Gopal, who had lived and died in a city three thousand miles away. Chandra provided many details about his former life that were later verified, and when he was taken to meet Gopal's relatives, he pointed the way to their house even though he had never been there. Similarly, in 1958 two-year-old Gnanatilleka of Sri Lanka described her life as a boy in a nearby village, and when she was taken to meet her former relatives, she was immediately able to identify them. By age seven, however, Gnanatilleka had forgotten her previous life.

A young boy whom followers believe to be the reincarnated Tibetan Lama.

The cases of Jagdish Chandra and Gnanatilleka were investigated by Dr. Ian Stevenson, a parapsychologist at the University of Virginia, whose research into reincarnation is the most thorough in the field. After studying dozens of reincarnation experiences, he was able to identify certain common aspects of the phenomenon.

Reincarnation is most often reported in countries where a belief in reincarnation is prevalent, such as India, although the phenomenon does occur elsewhere as well. The two lives involved in the reincarnation experience are usually of the same culture and live no farther than within one hundred miles of one another. Approximately three-fourths of the cases reported in India involve a person who can provide the name used in a former life, whereas in the United States only one-third of the experients can provide their previous name. Most experients claim to know how they died in their former life, and in most cases the death was violent. There is typically a space of time between this death and the experient's birthdate, ranging from weeks to years.

Most children who claim to remember a former life are between the ages of two and four, and between the ages of five and eight they stop remembering details of that former life. However, some experients later exhibit a phobia related to how they claim to have died in their previous life. For example, someone who said she died by drowning might have a serious, lifelong fear of water.

Stevenson's studies involve people who have remembered past lives spontaneously. Other researchers have examined memories of past lives that occur during hypnosis. In most cases these memories prove to be fantasies based on books the experient has read about life in other times. One person who remembered six former lives was later shown to have been recounting information from a variety of historical novels. In a few instances, the experients have exhibited knowledge similar to that of Stevenson's subjects.

Fraud, ESP, or possession?

People who do not believe that the spirit survives death offer several explanations for the reincarnation phenomenon. The first is fraud, particularly in cases where the experient would benefit from being associated with the past-life family. Stevenson agrees that fraud is possible; however, he does not believe that children as young as age two can be coached to lie so convincingly and in such detail.

Two other theories suggest that innocent error is involved. Perhaps witnesses are simply mistaken about the amount of past-life details provided by the experient, or the experient overheard those details before making any claims of a past life and incorporated them into a false reincarnation memory. Stevenson discounts these theories because of the number of cases in which the experient was able to recognize people he or she had never seen before.

A fourth theory is that the experient has telepathically received information about a deceased person from that person's relatives. However, Stevenson points out that the child claiming to have led a past life not only knows information about that life but also behaves similarly to the person who lived that former life. David H. Lund argues that ESP does not explain why a child would have information on only one other person's life:

> If the child is receiving the information via ESP, then why does he identify himself with a certain deceased person? And why does the information that he allegedly acquires by means of ESP seem to be limited to what that deceased person would have known? Why does he have ostensible memories of the life of only *that* person and not others?[37]

As a result of such questions, a fifth theory has been proposed: that the experient has actually been "possessed," or taken over, by the spirit of a deceased person. People who ascribe to this theory believe in ghosts and think that a malevolent spirit can take over an innocent person's body. Stevenson rejects this theory because it does not explain why the memories of a past life would gradually fade as the experient ages, or why a phobia related to the past-life death experience—drowning, for example—would linger.

As with OBEs and NDEs, acceptance or rejection of reincarnation experiences depends on a person's beliefs regarding the nature of the human spirit and its connection to the physical body. However, even some skeptics admit that more study is needed into such phenomena, if only to determine why so many people claim to have experienced them.

4

Spirits, Sprites, and Aliens

Extrasensory Perception (ESP), out-of-body experiences (OBEs), near-death experiences (NDEs), and reincarnation experiences are paranormal phenomena that rely on the abilities and memories of the experient. Another type of phenomenon places the experient in the role of observer. Ghost and UFO (unidentified flying object) sightings fall into this category, as do reports of personal encounters with such beings as aliens and fairies.

Apparitions and ghosts

Stories about ghosts have been told for centuries, and early investigators into paranormal phenomena sought to compile these stories, determine which ones seemed the most plausible, and categorize them. The Society for Psychical Research (SPR) published the first such work, including their "Census of Hallucinations," in 1894. Eventually investigators also sought to study ghosts firsthand, visiting the places where they were said to be found.

Modern researchers define a ghost as the image of a person, animal, or moving object that appears regularly in, or "haunts," a particular place. For example, there are several stories about ghost trains that pass along a particular stretch of railroad track on the anniversary of a train wreck. In contrast, apparitions are images of people or animals that are not tied to a particular place. An apparition of a man recently murdered, for example, might appear to several of his relatives living in different parts of the world.

Both apparitions and ghosts are usually perceived as solid, realistic figures rather than transparent ones, although they seem to pass through solid objects, and some cast shadows or have reflections in mirrors. Whereas ghosts of people are always said to look like someone who has died, apparitions are sometimes reported to represent someone who is dying, seriously ill, or undergoing some other trauma, such as a plane or car crash.

Researchers interviewing people who have seen apparitions or ghosts have identified several other differences between the two phenomena. Apparitions typically seem more aware of their surroundings than ghosts. An apparition might turn its head to follow a person's movements, for example, or walk around a chair to touch a particular object on a table. A ghost will often repeat the same actions over and over regardless of what objects are in a room or who is watching.

Ghost hunter Stephen Marshall holds a dowsing rod at a bridge, felt to be haunted by some area residents, near Hartford, Vermont. A train accident killed thirty-one people in 1887, and some people claim to see victims of the accident and hear the ill-fated crossing of the train.

Apparitions also tend to communicate with the experient, usually with gestures but sometimes in words. Stories abound about apparitions who revealed the location of hidden money or important documents or offered warnings that saved another person's life. Apparitions have told sailors to steer a different course, asked pilots to check for mechanical problems on their planes before taking off, and, in the case of murder victims, provided information that led to the capture of their killer. Apparitions typically continue to appear until their messages have been acted on, and then they are never seen again.

In contrast, ghosts often seem to have no goal and can haunt the same location for centuries. In most cases, the

A depiction of an apparition or a ghost; a difference between the two is that apparitions try to communicate a message, whereas ghosts seem to have no purpose.

place they haunt is somehow related to the death of the person the ghost appears to represent. One famous ghost story in Chicago, Illinois, concerns a hitchhiker known as Resurrection Mary. Young men driving along a particular route periodically encounter a young woman dressed in an old-fashioned party gown. When a driver pulls over to talk to her, she asks him for a ride home and gives her address, which he soon discovers is the location of the Resurrection Cemetery. Upon arriving at her destination, the young woman gets out of the car—either by opening the vehicle's door or passing through it—and walks up to the cemetery gates, where she vanishes. According to the locals, Mary was a young Polish woman killed on the road in 1931 while on her way home from a dance. She was buried in Resurrection Cemetery in her party gown.

Haunted houses

Far more common are stories involving ghosts who haunt houses. One of the most famous haunted houses is the Winchester House, now a tourist attraction in San Jose, California. The 160-room Victorian mansion was built by Sarah Winchester, who lived from 1840 to 1922. The family of Sarah's husband manufactured rifles, and Sarah believed that unless she continued to add rooms to her house she would be haunted by the ghosts of the people killed by the rifles.

After Sarah's death, stories began to circulate that she herself was haunting the house. A few people reported seeing a figure matching Sarah's description in various parts of the house, but more often experients claimed to hear unexplained sounds or smell unexplained odors. A caretaker heard breathing and footsteps, and a tour guide heard his name whispered. Two other tour guides smelled chicken soup where none was being cooked.

Other reports of haunting at the Winchester House involved the unexplained movement of objects. In their book *Historic Haunted America,* Michael Norman and Beth Scott recount the experiences of one employee:

> Some of the phenomena seem to be the product of a [ghost] bent on disrupting the staff's routine through puckish behavior.

The famous haunted Winchester House, where doors open unexplainably and appliances turn on randomly.

Allen Weitzel, a director of food and merchandising at Winchester House, was puzzled by several episodes. One night he locked all the doors to the gift shop and headed into a storeroom to set the alarm system. When he came back out, a glass door leading to the courtyard had somehow been unlocked. . . . About a year later, Weitzel was again by himself locking up for the night. He walked through the entire house turning off all the lights on the various tour routes. As he headed toward his car, he turned around to make sure he hadn't missed any. The house was dark. But when he reached his car and glanced back a final time, all the lights on the third floor were ablaze. . . . [On another occasion] Weitzel discovered his office soaked with water. . . . Everything from the paperwork on his desk to his chair and the floor was sopping wet. Even a pencil holder was filled with water. A light rain had fallen overnight, but not nearly enough to cause the extent of damage Weitzel found. And, most intriguing of all, the ceiling and walls were completely dry.[38]

Poltergeists

This kind of disruptive behavior is said to be caused by a poltergeist, a type of ghost that seems intent on causing trouble. Poltergeists are often connected to strange incidents related to water and sometimes to fire as well. When fire personnel investigate these fires, they can find no cause for them. Even more frequently, poltergeists make loud noises, move objects around, and can become violent with experients. Physical contact includes pushing, shoving, and pinching.

Many haunted house stories involve some degree of poltergeist behavior. There are also a few stories of poltergeists haunting a person instead of a house, following a specific individual around for days or even weeks. In his book *An Introduction to Parapsychology,* H. J. Irwin reports:

A séance is held for a young girl believed to be haunted by a poltergeist.

In mid-1965 unexplained movements of merchandise occurred in the chinaware department of a Bremen [Germany] store. Investigations by police and other authorities failed to establish any normal explanation for the events but they evidently were connected in some obscure way with a 15-year-old apprentice employee in the department. The lad was dismissed and the disturbances in the store immediately came to an end. The young man subsequently obtained a job as an apprentice in a Freiburg [Germany] electrical shop. In March 1966 he was asked to drill holes in a concrete wall and to install wall hooks. The task was done properly but a little later it was found that the hooks came loose in the presence of the young apprentice. He was accused of being to blame. In a test of this a freshly attached hook was observed to come loose within two minutes while the apprentice stood about a yard . . . from the wall.[39]

Psychokinesis

In studying incidents where poltergeists seemed to haunt one particular person, investigators realized that many of the experients involved were emotionally troubled adolescents. In one study, approximately 62 percent of experients were under age eighteen and living away from home when the poltergeist activities began. H. J. Irwin notes that "this suggests that poltergeist disturbances in some way are associated with emotional conflict in the focal person. The frequency of adolescent cases may indicate further that the [experient] is not in a position to express the conflict openly."[40]

Some researchers theorize that poltergeists are actually cases of psychokinesis (PK), a type of psychic ability that enables the experient to move objects. There have been cases of people who appear able to move or bend objects at will, although skeptics have called all such cases fraudulent. Parapsychologists suggest that perhaps poltergeist experients are also able to move objects, but subconsciously rather than at will, as a way to relieve emotional tension.

Researchers have developed several ways to test an experient's ability to move objects again and again without obvious effort, a phenomenon called recurrent spontaneous psychokinesis (RSPK). One of the most common methods is to have the experient roll dice, typically using an electric dice-tumbling machine rather than the hands, with the goal of making the dice show certain numerical combinations. People associated with incidents of RSPK typically roll the correct numbers at a rate higher than chance, but skeptics do not accept this as proof that PK exists.

Moreover, RSPK does not explain poltergeist experiences that center on places rather than people. In these cases, the most frequently proposed theory is that poltergeists—as well as ghosts and apparitions—are the surviving consciousness of the dead. But as with OBEs, NDEs, and reincarnation experiences, skeptics insist that the spirit does not survive the death of the physical body, and point out that even if it did, it would not need to wear clothes, as

ghosts do. Skeptics further argue that all hauntings can be explained as frauds, embellished stories, misinterpretations of natural events, or hallucinations.

Some evidence seems to support the view that apparitions are hallucinations. Although these images appear solid, experients can put their hands through them. Apparitions also leave behind no physical evidence, such as footprints, and often an object that the experient thought was moved by the apparition turns out not to have been. Perhaps more importantly, when a group of people are involved in an apparition sighting, not everyone present can see the image, suggesting that the event is an internal one rather than an external one.

But while some parapsychologists agree with skeptics that apparitions are created in the mind of the experient, they dispute that these images are simple hallucinations. Instead they propose that the experient is projecting the ghostly images through some form of mental telepathy. Various theories incorporating this view have been developed over the years, including the idea that telepathy can be "contagious," meaning that one person can acquire an image through telepathy and then transmit it to others, so many people visiting a haunted house will see the same image.

UFOs

Similar theories have been proposed to explain UFO sightings. Many parapsychologists suggest that these sightings are caused by some form of mental telepathy that projects images into the sky or transmits them from one person to another, while skeptics believe these images to be hallucinations or frauds. Meanwhile, according to polls conducted by major news organizations, a majority of the public now believes that UFOs are alien spacecraft from distant planets.

This belief is supported by the fact that many photographs and videotapes seem to show UFOs in flight. Skeptics believe that these photos have been faked or represent natural objects or phenomena, such as airplanes or reflections of light, that have been misinterpreted. Believers counter that photo experts have declared many of these pictures authentic and fault skeptics for denying what

seems to them to be the simplest explanation for the photos: UFOs really are alien spacecraft.

People who support the idea that UFOs represent contact with alien life believe that the U.S. government has been hiding evidence of this fact for years. The event most commonly cited as proof of the government's concealment is the Roswell incident. On July 2, 1947, there was a violent thunderstorm in the area around the army airfield in Roswell, New Mexico. The next day, rancher Mac Brazel found hundreds of pieces of a strange tinfoil-like material in one of his fields. Some of the pieces were shaped like I-beams, which are horizontal girders used in building construction. Most were extremely lightweight and thin but could not be bent, cut, or burned.

Suspecting the pieces might have come from the crash of an experimental military aircraft, Brazel took some of them to the local sheriff, who called officials at the airfield. Officers sent two military intelligence agents to investigate

A photograph depicting a UFO flying low over the treeline.

the matter. One of them, Jesse A. Marcel, quickly became convinced that the pieces were debris from a crashed alien spacecraft, and he retained this view for the rest of his life.

After Marcel gave samples of the debris to his superior officers, the military ordered him not to tell anyone what he had found. The government then announced that the debris was from an ordinary weather balloon, and invited reporters who had heard rumors of an alien crash to come to the military base to photograph the debris. According to Marcel, the debris the officials showed reporters was not the same debris he had seen in the field.

Meanwhile, military personnel were sent to search the area where the debris was originally discovered, and some of these men later claimed they found alien bodies a short distance from the wreckage. Other people have reported seeing the alien bodies at a military hospital and on an airplane that transported the bodies to another military base. In fact, more than 350 people eventually said they saw the alien bodies, and others said they worked with materials from the alien spacecraft.

The government has always denied that any of these stories are true. Nonetheless, the Roswell incident fueled the

A photograph from the Air Force's "Roswell Report" showing insulated bags reportedly holding temperature-sensitive test dummies. Some, however, believe the bags to contain the bodies of aliens.

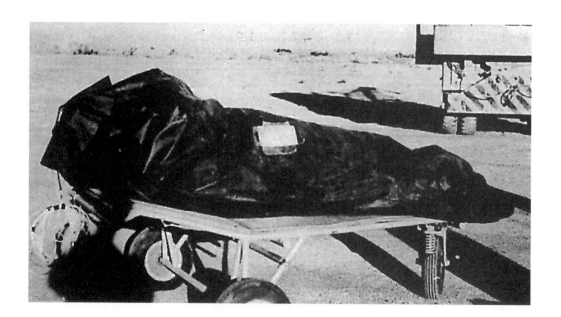

public's belief that UFOs are alien spacecraft. Thousands of people have witnessed unexplained objects in the sky and insist that these could not be mere hallucinations or telepathic experiences.

Alien abductions

Some people also claim to have been forcibly taken, or abducted, by the occupants of UFOs. Known as abductees, these people offer remarkably similar stories about their experiences. All of them report being taken from an isolated location, whether a deserted road, a forest, or a private home, with no one else around. Some abductees went to these places by choice, but others report being drawn to them by a sudden, inexplicable urge.

Most abductees are alone, but others are in small groups. In either case, the abductees see a UFO and encounter an alien, which they describe as having a large head and enormous black eyes. Abductees also report that the aliens have no hair and are milky white in color, but they disagree on whether the aliens have ears and noses. Mouths are typically described as either slitlike with no lips or O-shaped with very thin lips, but regardless of their shape, these mouths are not used for talking. Almost all abductees say that aliens communicate telepathically.

In most abduction stories, when an alien approaches the abductee, the abductee suddenly falls into a trancelike state. The alien then takes the abductee into the spaceship, down a dark tunnel, and into a brightly lit room and performs a variety of medical experiments on the person's body. Afterward the abductee is returned to the site of the abduction, usually without a memory of what happened. However, the abductee is aware of an unexplained loss of time, and memories of the event often resurface later, either spontaneously or through hypnosis.

Some abductees also exhibit physical signs of the experience. Some have small or faded scars that they claim were the result of medical experiments, while others exhibit signs of having been someplace they do not

Abductee Charles Hickson shows the spot on the Pascagola River in Mississippi where he claims to have been abducted by aliens in 1973.

remember visiting. Abductee Clare Holcomb describes her experience:

> I was abducted from my bedroom. I had on a nightgown and no shoes. Naturally, I didn't sleep in my shoes. And when I was brought back, the aliens made a mistake. Instead of putting me back in the house, they left me outside. We'd had severe ice storms, and it was bitter cold. I couldn't get in the house. The doors were locked. The garage door was frozen shut, and I couldn't get it open. I was standing on frozen gravel with about an inch of ice on it, and my feet adhered to the ice. I thought I was going to die because they wouldn't find me until morning. When I started thinking about death, the aliens came back, picked me up and put me back in the house. The next morning, all the skin on the bottom of my feet had been burned off from sticking to the ice.[41]

A psychological phenomenon

Skeptics would suggest that Holcomb was sleepwalking, and they dismiss abductee scars as being the result of minor accidents or childhood injuries long forgotten. Researchers into the phenomenon report that none of the physical evidence has yet been unequivocal. In his book *Unexplained!* Jerome Clark points out that

> Abduction reports, like other high-strangeness narratives, make the most extraordinary sorts of claims in support of which they produce only circumstantial evidence. Such evidence, which never rises above the consistent-with-the-hypothesis variety, ranges from unaccounted-for marks on abductees' bodies to patterns in the data [commonalities in the stories] that appear explainable neither by chance nor by cultural contamination [i.e., hearing the stories of other experients]. Few knowledgeable investigators, whether ufologists or mental-health professionals, doubt that the abduction phenomenon is an enigma; neither would many argue that the evidence so far available is sufficient to do anything more than keep the question open.[42]

Meanwhile, abductees' descriptions of the tunnel and bright light remind parapsychologists of descriptions given by subjects who reported an NDE. Skeptics interpret this as proof that abductees are having some form of hallucination, fantasy, or memory of the birth process. But some NDE researchers argue that this means the NDE subjects and abductees have both gone through some kind of mental transformation that allows them to see the same place— an imaginal realm with otherworldly beings that could be construed as either angels or aliens. A few researchers even suggest that this place is real, but that it exists in a different dimension than the real world.

Others believe that aliens are the product of ordinary dreams. Psychiatrist Carl Jung studied people's dreams and discovered that they all contain the same basic images, regardless of the person's culture. He called these common images "archetypes" and said that they symbolize humanity's deepest desires and fears. Jung theorized that all people experience the same archetypes because all people have the same ancestral memories, which are passed on from generation to generation through the genes, just as eye color and hair color are passed on. Jung called these ancient, shared memories the "collective unconscious."

Jung related the collective unconscious to the abduction phenomenon in his 1959 book *Flying Saucers: A Modern Myth,* saying that abductees might not be seeing real aliens but archetypal images. In other words, abduction stories are symbolic dreams that reflect emotions and communal memories.

Fairies

Some researchers reject Jung's theory because aliens are a modern concept that did not exist in ancient times. Jung's supporters say that aliens are just an updated version of the fairy, an otherworldly being that has been discussed in stories for centuries. Fairies were often said to steal children away, as did other legendary creatures like elves, trolls, and gnomes. Perhaps all of these creatures were images of the collective unconscious.

Abductee Whitley Strieber, who has written about his experiences in several books, suggests that fairies, elves, and similar beings might have been real creatures. This view is not widespread today, but at one time many people believed in fairies and elves. In fact, between 1917 and 1921 there was a rash of fairy sightings, many of them investigated by Sir Arthur Conan Doyle, who was best known as the author who created the character of Sherlock Holmes.

The most famous fairy sighting that Doyle investigated occurred in 1917 in the village of Cottingley in Yorkshire, England. Two cousins, sixteen-year-old Elsie Wright and ten-year-old Frances Griffiths, claimed that they saw fairies while playing in a glen near Elsie's house. To prove their claim, they borrowed a camera and took a picture of the fairies. It showed Frances standing behind five winged fairies that stood approximately six inches tall. The girls took a second photograph a month later, this time of a single gnomelike fairy.

For a time the photographs remained a family curiosity. Then in 1919 Elsie's mother attended a lecture on fairies and shared the pictures with the group. Her photographs soon came to the attention of Doyle, who published them along with an article in *Strand* magazine in 1920. Mean-

Sir Arthur Conan Doyle writing at his desk.

while, the girls took three more pictures of fairies; these were published in *Strand* magazine in 1921.

Photo experts examined the pictures and pronounced them real, although one of them acknowledged that a skilled adult might have been able to fake them. For most of their lives Frances and Elsie insisted they had not fabricated the photographs. Then in 1972, Elsie said the pictures were a hoax. Four years later, she once again said they were real. But in 1983, the two cousins said that Elsie had drawn the fairies, using pictures in a children's book entitled *Princess Mary's Gift Book,* and then posed and photographed them, although they never explained their techniques.

Because the pictures were authenticated when they first appeared, many people accepted them as real, and this in turn contributed to the public's belief in fairies. Similarly, once the media began publishing UFO photographs, more people professed a belief in UFOs. Other unexplained

Scientists deploy a "creature camera" to search for the famous Loch Ness monster.

creatures, such as the Loch Ness monster said to inhabit the Scottish lake called Loch Ness, have also gained credibility from photographic evidence, even when the evidence has not proved to be authentic.

But many beliefs are not predicated on hard evidence. Few people have claimed to have photographs of ghosts, yet most people believe in them. And while there are no photographs of angels, a majority of the American public is convinced they are real. As reporter John Stossel points out in his ABC television special "The Power of Belief," some beliefs are a matter of faith.

> Usually, before we'll believe something, we want proof. Or as much proof as we can get. Before you buy a car, you try to check it out. Before I'll try to skate across that frozen lake, I'm going to make sure the ice is solid. But when it comes to the supernatural, ESP, psychic powers, astrology and so forth, lots of people have a different standard. They believe because they want to believe. They care less about proof because believing makes them happy.[43]

5

A Matter of Faith

A BELIEF IN ghosts, aliens, or telepathy is not dependent on a person's religious faith. However, other paranormal phenomena do attract believers of one particular faith or another. For example, believers in angels, miracles, stigmata, and faith healing are generally Christians who are convinced that such phenomena are the works of God.

Angels

Surveys indicate that most Americans—even those who do not attend church regularly—believe in angels. Although angels were mentioned in the Bible, the modern version of these heavenly beings is quite different from the one presented in ancient writings. The Bible portrays angels as powerful, sword-wielding, fearless, and frightening. Modern angels are kind, helpful, and rather innocuous. In a 1993 *Time* magazine article about the angel phenomenon, reporter Nancy Gibbs notes that today's angels are all "guardian angels" who protect people, whereas in ancient times angels typically brought people life-changing messages from God or influenced the outcome of wars.

> In their modern incarnation, these mighty messengers and fearless soldiers have been reduced to bite-size beings, easily digested. The terrifying cherubim have become Kewpie-doll cherubs. For those who choke too easily on God and his rules, theologians observe, angels are the handy compromise, all fluff and meringue, kind, nonjudgmental. And they are available to everyone, like aspirin.[44]

Ancient writings portray angels as powerful and sword-wielding, as seen in this statue.

Stories about guardian angels have been published in several recent books. The stories often involve a mysterious stranger who shows up to offer help and comfort; afterward experients decide that the stranger must have been a guardian angel. In her book *A Book of Angels*, Sophy Burnham writes about one such story.

I have a friend, Jack Moorman, an investment banker. . . . When he was eight years old, he was alone in the house one day, woodworking with his new set of ultra-sharp cutting tools, when the knife slipped. It cut his finger to the quick. . . . At that moment, the doorbell rang. Wrapping his hand in a towel, he opened the door. It was a nurse in a white uniform asking for his parents. He says now, forty years later, that he never thought it was strange to see a nurse at the door for no reason. She came inside, cleaned his wound, bandaged his hand, and left. She never returned. He never did learn why she'd really come. It is only now, four decades later, that he recognizes how strange was the encounter. Was she an angel come to minister to him, being all alone?[45]

In other stories, angels appear to experients as other-worldly beings, which in no way can be mistaken for regular human beings. Burnham tells the story of Hope MacDonald's encounter with an angel:

> Her sister, Marilyn, was eight at the time and Hope herself was four when her parents drove Marilyn as usual to school one day. An hour later she watched as they carried her big sister back into the house covered with bruises and blood. They put her on the sofa until the doctor arrived. It seems that in crossing the street to school, Marilyn had darted in front of a car and been hit and tossed high in the air. Her parents watched helplessly as she hit the pavement and rolled over and over toward a large, uncovered, open sewer. But instead of falling in, as expected, she suddenly stopped, right at the lip of the sewer.

As depicted by this marble angel, people today tend to view angels as kind, helpful, and attractive.

Her parents told this story to the doctor, and they all shook their heads in amazement. How could the child have stopped so suddenly, at the very edge of the sewer, when she had been rolling so fast?

In a voice filled with surprise, Marilyn spoke up from the sofa and said, "But didn't you see that huge, beautiful angel standing in the sewer, holding up her hands to keep me from rolling in?"[46]

Heavenly beings, hallucinations, or ghosts?

In many such stories, only one person out of those present actually sees the angel. Skeptics say this is because the sighting is a hallucination on the part of the experient, arguing that if angels were real then more people would see them. Believers insist that skeptics would see angels too, if only they had enough faith. Rev. John Westerhoff, a theologian at Duke University, says,

Angels exist through the eyes of faith, and faith is perception. Only if you can perceive it can you experience it. For some, their faith doesn't have room for such creatures. That's not to demean their faith. That's just the way they are; they can't believe in things that aren't literal, that are outside the five senses.[47]

But skeptics point out that many angel sightings take place when the experient is undergoing some kind of trauma. As Gibbs notes, "the experiences of angelic presence seem to occur most often in moments of heightened awareness—when everyday life has already been disrupted by some pressing fear or obstacle."[48] Skeptics argue that this supports their theory that angel sightings are hallucinations, which they attribute to stress- or fatigue-related psychological phenomena.

Even people who believe in paranormal phenomena sometimes have trouble accepting the existence of angels because this acceptance is related to religious faith. This type of skeptic suggests that angels are really ghosts who have been mistaken for heavenly beings. But stories related to ghost and angel sightings describe important differences between the two. Sophy Burnham, who claims to have seen both angels and ghosts, explains the differences:

When a spirit enters a room, you feel a chill, as if a door's been left ajar, and when it touches you or when its body passes through you, you feel an arctic cold. . . . But angels are different, and no one who has seen an angel ever mistakes it for a ghost. Angels are remarkable for their warmth and light, and all who see them speak in awe of their iridescent and refulgent light, of brilliant colors, or else of the unbearable whiteness of their being. You are flooded with laughter, happiness. . . . Angels give aid, or bring messages of hope, but what they do *not* do is wander, earthbound, like the lonely spirits who are dead.[49]

Miracles

The same argument is also applied to miracles: Are they illusions or are they real? And if they are real, are they truly

Candles burn beside a statue of the Virgin Mary. Many miracles are perceived by those of the Catholic faith.

related to God? A miracle is a positive event that cannot be explained in terms of any known reality. One example is a visible affirmation of faith, such as when people see the shape of the Virgin Mary in candle drippings or tree bark, or when a religious statue appears to be weeping tears or shedding blood. In 1953 a plaster statue of the Virgin Mary in Syracuse, Italy, "cried" for over a month, and in 1968 a three-hundred-year-old wooden cross in Pôrto Alegre, Brazil, began exuding a red substance that many believed was blood. Many people witnessed the events, and according to scientists of the time, the tears and blood were real.

Skeptics dismiss such events as hoaxes or cases of spontaneous or drug-induced hallucination. Most deny even the possibility that a miracle might occur. In this respect, they share the view of Cicero, a Roman statesman who lived from 106 to 43 B.C. He once said, "Nothing happens without a cause, and nothing happens unless it can happen. When that which can happen does in fact happen, it cannot be considered a miracle. Hence, there are no miracles."[50]

But most people do not share this view, particularly where episodes of divine intervention are concerned. A divine intervention occurs when someone's life is saved through an event that seems beyond coincidence. One example of such an event is the case of John Lee, who was sentenced to hang for murder in 1885. The execution was attempted four times, and four times the trapdoor of the gallows refused to open. In between each attempt, various people tried to figure out why the trapdoor had jammed, but in every test of the mechanism it worked perfectly. Eventually Lee's sentence was commuted to life in prison, and after twenty-two years he was released on parole.

Many explanations have been offered for what happened to Lee, including the possibilities that rainwater had swelled the trapdoor and that the builder had rigged the gallows so it would not work. Each of these theories was considered at the time the equipment was being tested, and none proved to be true. Skeptics, however, have declared that such events are due to luck or coincidence, believing that no divine hand has been involved in them. If any hand was involved at all, they say, it was the hand of a human trying to trick others into believing in miracles.

Faith healing

This is also how skeptics explain another type of miracle, faith healing, which involves spontaneous cures supposedly brought about by prayer. In many cases, faith healing is accomplished through the touch of a person who claims the ability to heal the sick in the name of God. Skeptics believe that such people are either intentionally trying to trick others, whether for profit or self-aggrandizement, or imagining their own powers. Skeptic Joe Nickell, who has studied faith healing, believes the latter is more common. He says

While others watch, a modern faith healer prays over a patient.

that "the people who make the claims are rational, but may have a higher fantasy quotient than others."[51]

Moreover, skeptics say that whether or not a faith healer is involved, spontaneous cures through prayer are caused by a positive mental attitude rather than by God. Physicians have long known that the human mind can affect the body's health. For example, scientific studies have shown that prayer and meditation can reduce blood pressure and that religious people tend to recover more quickly from surgery. Doctors believe that similar forces might be at work when a person's cancer suddenly goes into remission, even though medical treatments have failed.

Even people who study miracles for the Catholic Church agree that many spontaneous cures can be explained by psychology if not by medical science. One of these people, Dr. Ennio Ensoli, says, "Sometimes we have cases that you could call exceptional, but that's not enough. Exceptional doesn't mean inexplicable."[52] Since 1989, the Catholic Church has deemed only one spontaneous cure a miracle.

The Lourdes miracles

That one case occurred in Lourdes, a city near Paris, France, where a sixty-nine-year-old man visited a shrine and later found he could walk for the first time in three years. The Lourdes shrine is in a grotto where, in 1858, a young girl named Bernadette Soubirous saw visions of the Virgin Mary. Bernadette's first vision occurred one day while she and two other girls were gathering firewood near the Gave de Pau stream. Separated from her companions, Bernadette saw the Virgin Mary in the grotto, and after nine subsequent visions in the same place, she discovered that there was a spring in the grotto. Shortly thereafter, a blind man bathed in the water and reported that it had restored his sight.

Bernadette had nearly twenty visions in all, and by the sixteenth one, the grotto had become famous as a place for cures. By 1883 the Catholic Church had established a medical board to investigate the Lourdes miracles, and this board deemed many of the cures authentic. Today approxi-

mately 3 million people visit the site each year seeking cures for a variety of ailments.

But skeptics believe that the church was wrong in deciding that the most recent Lourdes cure was a true miracle. According to the church, the man who was unable to walk had "an organic infection similar to multiple sclerosis in a severe and advanced stage, of which the sudden cure during a pilgrimage to Lourdes [is] unusual and inexplicable according to all the knowledge of science."[53] Skeptics argue that just because his cure could not be explained at the time does not mean it defies explanation. Perhaps his

The grotto in Lourdes, France, where a vision of the Virgin Mary appeared to a young girl in 1858.

disease was simply misdiagnosed, or perhaps doctors were mistaken in believing he would not recover on his own.

Similarly, author Ted Harrison argues that although many miracles seem to defy logic, they might still be explained given enough time and scientific progress. In his book *Stigmata,* Harrison writes:

> It could well be that some of the miracles associated with mystical phenomena . . . could be reinterpreted, and that it might be shown one day that the human being undergoing a profound religious experience can have an effect on the physical world. It is now no longer a mystery to us that electromagnetic forces exist, and magnetism and radio waves can be very precisely harnessed. There is still much to learn about the universe.[54]

Stigmata

Stigmata is a type of miracle in which a person spontaneously exhibits physical marks that represent the suffering Jesus Christ experienced during his crucifixion. The marks include wounds on the hands and feet much like those Christ might have developed when nails were hammered through his hands and feet; a wound on the side as though the experient has been stabbed the way Christ was; and scratches on the head similar to those made by Christ's crown of thorns. In many cases, visions of Christ accompany the stigmata experience.

Harrison offers several modern examples of the stigmata phenomenon, including the case of Heather Woods, a forty-three-year-old British woman. In May 1992, Woods "found small itching blisters in her hands developed into large round tender areas of skin which periodically seeped blood. Similar marks appeared on her feet and a red crescent appeared on her right side. Twice a red mark has appeared on her forehead in the distinct shape of a cross."[55] Harrison notes that

> the history of Christianity is full of stories of miracles, wonder and mystery. Many of the stories require deep faith to be believed and so can be dismissed by the cynic with ease. The stigmata have taken many forms and have appeared in a variety of ways, and while a sceptic [skeptic] can deny that the marks have anything to do with God and can maintain that they appear only

A painting of Saint Francis of Assisi receiving stigmata, or wounds of Christ.

on hysterical or unbalanced subjects and are possibly self-inflicted, what cannot be denied is that they exist physically and tangibly.[56]

Most physicians view stigmata as a psychological phenomenon, much like faith healing. There is ample proof that the mind can physically change the body, not only internally but externally as well. For example, the mind can cause the face to blush and the body to develop rashes and hives. In some documented cases, the mind can create even more dramatic physical transformations, as Harrison reports:

In the medical journal *The Lancet* of December 28th, 1946 a case was described of a thirty-five-year-old man who, while under close observation in hospital, had produced wounds on his arms corresponding to the rope marks he had received nine years earlier when being forcibly restrained. The marks were clear indentations which also bled. His doctor concluded that there was no way to describe what he had seen as other than a 'genuine psychosomatic phenomenon'. When the marks had appeared the patient had seemed to be severely disturbed, reliving in his mind and in his actions the original experience which had caused the injuries.[57]

Harrison writes of several similar incidents, including one in which a doctor actually induced a patient to develop such wounds during hypnosis. He told her that a crown of thorns had been put on her head, and within an hour bloody spots appeared where the thorns might have scratched her. People who do not believe in paranormal

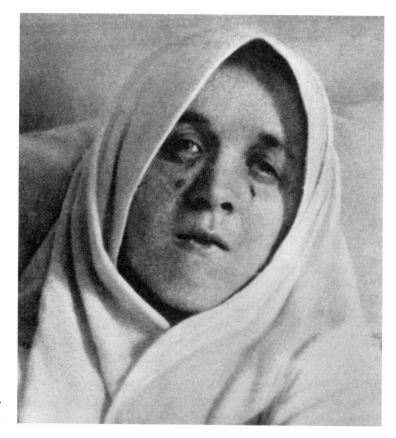

Therese Neumann, a Catholic who shows what some believe to be the wounds of stigmata.

phenomena, religious or otherwise, say this is proof that the human mind is capable of producing a wide variety of physical experiences, and they have compared stigmata to the wounds exhibited by people who claim to have been abducted by aliens.

Miracles without human involvement

But some miracles do not allow for the possibility of human involvement and are therefore not subject to psychological explanations. In his book *Beyond Reason,* Baptist clergyman Pat Robertson tells the story of a man who prayed for a miracle of nature:

> Back in 1977, unusual weather conditions threatened to destroy the orange groves in Norvell Hayes's part of Florida. The trees in the area were covered with icicles, and the orange growers knew from past experience that it was highly likely that the cold would kill their crops. But Norvell wasn't willing to accept the disaster that seemed inevitable. He believed God could save his trees, and he asked for a miracle.
>
> "I got in my car, drove to the orange grove, and parked along the highway," he said. "I just looked at the grove and . . . [prayed for it to be spared]." A few weeks later, the sun began to shine again and things warmed up. Norvell still gets excited when he describes the result of his prayer. "Fruit was developing on my trees! The twenty-five hundred orange trees on the property across the road, which was owned by another grower, were dead. But on my side of the road, it was different. It was as though a shield had been placed on my property line, which stopped the potentially damaging frost from crossing it. I didn't lose a tree."[58]

Should life be explainable?

Skeptics might say that this is merely a story, but the faithful believe it is proof that God exists. Moreover, Rev. Peter Gomes, a minister at Harvard University's Memorial Church, wonders why some people are so determined to explain or dismiss such events: "It dulls the imagination if you have an explanation for everything. We've become so explanation-oriented in our culture, we've lost the sense of the transcendent."[59]

Similarly, Dan Wakefield, author of *Expect a Miracle: The Miraculous Things That Happen to Ordinary People,* says, "The more science discovers, the more secrets there are to see in the structure and meaning of the universe. People are disillusioned with rational answers. They realize there is another dimension to life."[60] In other words, not everything can be explained, nor should it be.

Meanwhile, skeptics insist that every paranormal phenomenon has a logical, scientific explanation, even though that explanation might not be known at the present time; they argue that it is better for people to believe only in phenomena that have been proven real. John Stossel, in his ABC television special "The Power of Faith," says, "The real world's all we've got. Believers in the supernatural claim to have special wisdom about the world. But real wisdom means knowing truth from falsehood, knowing the difference between evidence and wishful thinking."[61]

Paranormal phenomena are mysteries that might someday be explained, so people will no longer argue about whether or not they are real. The question is whether people truly *want* all of life's mysteries explained. As skeptic Champe Ransom acknowledges in discussing children's belief in Santa Claus:

> [There] is a fear that questioning and searching will destroy wonder. . . . It is a fear that romance and wonder and love will not survive, ultimately, once we begin to lose a belief in, say, angels. . . . It is a feeling that, if we lose the ability to imagine wondrous, unseen things, and to consider them as possibly real, we lose a delightful and very important capacity.[62]

Notes

Introduction

1. Jerome Clark, *Unexplained!* Detroit: Visible Ink, 1999, p. xi.
2. Clark, *Unexplained!* pp. xiv–xv.
3. Clark, *Unexplained!* p. xxv.

Chapter 1: Psychic Connections

4. Paul Chambers, *Paranormal People.* London: Blandford, 1998, p. 184.
5. Richard S. Broughton, *Parapsychology: The Controversial Science.* New York: Ballantine Books, 1991, p. 68.
6. Milbourne Christopher, *ESP, Seers, and Psychics: What the Occult Really Is.* New York: Crowell, 1979, pp. 37–38.
7. Quoted in Broughton, *Parapsychology: The Controversial Science,* p. 17.
8. Quoted in David L. Bender and Bruno Leone, eds., *Paranormal Phenomena: Opposing Viewpoints.* San Diego: Greenhaven Press, 1997, p. 141.
9. Arthur Lyons and Marcello Truzzi, *The Blue Sense: Psychic Detectives and Crime.* New York: Mysterious Press, 1991, p. 32.
10. Lyons and Truzzi, *The Blue Sense,* pp. 1–2.
11. Lyons and Truzzi, *The Blue Sense,* p. 3.

Chapter 2: Predicting the Future: Psychic Ability or Gullibility?

12. Broughton, *Parapsychology: The Controversial Science,* p. 8.
13. Chambers, *Paranormal People,* p. 37.
14. Broughton, *Parapsychology: The Controversial Science,* p. 23.
15. Broughton, *Parapsychology: The Controversial Science,* p. 24.
16. Broughton, *Parapsychology: The Controversial Science,* pp. 21–22.
17. Quoted in Reader's Digest Association, *Mysteries of the Unexplained.* Pleasantville, NY: Reader's Digest Books, 1984, p. 16.
18. Quoted in Reader's Digest Association, *Mysteries of the Unexplained,* p. 16.

19. Quoted in Reader's Digest Association, *Mysteries of the Unexplained,* p. 17.

20. Quoted in Chambers, *Paranormal People,* p. 25.

21. Chambers, *Paranormal People,* p. 25.

22. George O. Abell and Barry Singer, eds., *Science and the Paranormal: Probing the Existence of the Supernatural.* New York: Charles Scribner's Sons, 1981, p. 88.

23. "The Power of Belief," hosted by John Stossel. Transcript of ABCNews Special, aired October 6, 1998, p. 17.

24. Sylvia Brown and Antoinette May, *Adventures of a Psychic.* Carlsbad, CA: Hay House, 1998, pp. 91–92.

25. "The Power of Belief," ABCNews Special, p. 13.

26. "The Power of Belief," ABCNews Special, pp. 13–14.

Chapter 3: Altered States: The Mind/Body Connection

27. Roger Highfield, "The Hypnotic State Remains a Phenomenon That Divides the Experts," *Daily Telegraph,* August 15, 1998.

28. Quoted in Kenneth Frazier, ed., *Paranormal Borderlands of Science.* Buffalo, NY: Prometheus Books, 1981, p. 162.

29. Melvin Morse with Paul Perry, *Closer to the Light: Learning from the Near-Death Experiences of Children.* New York: Villard Books, 1990, p. 106.

30. Broughton, *Parapsychology: The Controversial Science,* p. 244.

31. Quoted in Morse, *Closer to the Light,* pp. 37–38.

32. Morse, *Closer to the Light,* p. 38.

33. Quoted in H. J. Irwin, *An Introduction to Parapsychology.* Jefferson, NC: McFarland, 1989, p. 191.

34. Quoted in Broughton, *Parapsychology: The Controversial Science,* p. 255.

35. Morse, *Closer to the Light,* pp. 117–18.

36. Quoted in Morse, *Closer to the Light,* p. 111.

37. David H. Lund, *Death and Consciousness.* Jefferson, NC: McFarland, 1985, p. 165.

Chapter 4: Spirits, Sprites, and Aliens

38. Michael Norman and Beth Scott, *Historic Haunted America.* New York: Tor, 1995, pp. 49–50.

39. Irwin, *An Introduction to Parapsychology,* pp. 175–76.

40. Irwin, *An Introduction to Parapsychology,* p. 176.

41. Quoted in Susan Michaels, *Sightings: UFOs.* New York: Simon & Schuster, 1997, p. 194.

42. Clark, *Unexplained!* p. xxi.

43. "The Power of Belief," ABCNews Special, pp. 1–2.

Chapter 5: A Matter of Faith

44. Nancy Gibbs, "Angels Among Us," *Time,* December 27, 1993, p. 56.

45. Sophy Burnham, *A Book of Angels.* New York: Ballantine Books, 1990, pp. 47–48.

46. Burnham, *A Book of Angels,* pp. 36–37.

47. Quoted in Gibbs, "Angels Among Us," p. 57.

48. Gibbs, "Angels Among Us," p. 57.

49. Burnham, *A Book of Angels,* pp. 23–24.

50. Quoted in Lance Morrow, "How to Believe in Miracles," *Time,* December 30, 1991, p. 68.

51. Quoted in Bill Roberts, "The Growing Mystery of Faith Healing," Gannet News Service, December 29, 1995.

52. Quoted in David Van Biema, "Modern Miracles Have Strict Rules," *Time,* April 10, 1995, p. 72.

53. Quoted in Julie Wheelwright, "Friday Book: A Place for Belief in Miracles," *Independent,* April 2, 1999, p. 5.

54. Ted Harrison, *Stigmata: A Medieval Phenomenon in a Modern Age.* New York: St. Martin's Press, 1994, p. 143.

55. Harrison, *Stigmata,* pp. 1–2.

56. Harrison, *Stigmata,* p. 3.

57. Harrison, *Stigmata,* pp. 11–12.

58. Pat Robertson, *Beyond Reason: How Miracles Can Change Your Life.* New York: William Morrow, 1985, pp. 11–12.

59. Quoted in Diane Winston, "The Wonder of Miracles," *Dallas Morning News,* March 29, 1997, p. 1G.

60. Quoted in Winston, "The Wonder of Miracles," p. 1G.

61. "The Power of Belief," ABCNews Special, p. 21.

62. Champe Ransom, "Yes, Virginia, There Probably Is No Santa Claus," *Humanist,* vol. 57, November 21, 1997, p. 33.

Organizations
to Contact

AngelWatch
P.O. Box 1362
Mountainside, NJ 07092

Dedicated to sharing stories of angel encounters, this group publishes a bimonthly magazine; its founder, Eileen Elias Freeman, gives workshops on spirituality, angels, and the power of prayer.

Committee for the Scientific Investigation of Claims of the Paranormal (CSICOP)
P.O. Box 703
Amherst, NY 14226
(716) 636-1425
e-mail: Skeptinq@aol.com

Supported by psychologists, astronomers, physicists, and other scientists interested in paranormal phenomena, this organization holds conferences and symposiums on a wide variety of subjects, including UFOs, ESP, alien abduction, and ghosts. The group publishes a bimonthly magazine, the *Skeptical Inquirer.* Its literature promotes "the need to question everything" and says that "the real world is far more exciting than anything the wishful thinkers can come up with."

J. Allan Hyneck Center for UFO Studies (CUFOS)
2457 W. Peterson Ave., Suite 6
Chicago, IL 60659
(312) 271-3611

This organization sponsors scientific research into and disseminates information about a variety of UFO-related phenomena. The group produces two publications, the quarterly *International UFO Reporter* and the annual *Journal of UFO Studies.*

Mutual UFO Network (MUFON)
103 Oldtowne Rd.
Seguin, TX 78155
(210) 379-9216
website: www.rutgers.edu/~mcgrew/mufon/index.html

Founded in 1969, this organization is now one of the most influential UFO groups in the United States. It investigates UFO sightings throughout the world. Its members include scientists, psychologists, and military personnel. The group produces three publications: the *MUFON Field Investigators Manual,* which appears five times a year; the *MUFON International UFO Symposium Proceedings,* which appears once a year; and the *MUFON UFO Journal,* which appears once a month.

The Program for Extraordinary Experience Research (PEER)
P.O. Box 382427
Cambridge, MA 02238-2427
(617) 497-5781

This nonprofit research and education group investigates a variety of "extraordinary experiences," including alien abductions and ghost sightings.

The Seti Institute
2035 Landings Dr.
Mountain View, CA 94043
(650) 961-6633
website: www.seti-inst.edu/

The Seti Institute supports a variety of scientific research projects related to searching for intelligent extraterrestrial life. It also sponsors education programs on UFOs and other subjects related to life in the universe.

Skeptics Society
P.O. Box 338
Altadena, CA 91001
(818) 794-3119

This organization investigates paranormal phenomena and publishes the quarterly magazine *Skeptic*. Its board members include noted skeptic James Randi, who has debunked a variety of claims related to the paranormal. The group's literature quotes the philosophy of seventeenth-century Dutch philosopher Baruch Spinoza: "I have made a ceaseless effort not to ridicule, not to bewail, not to scorn human actions, but to understand them."

Society for Psychical Research (SPR)
49 Marloes Rd.
Kensington, London W8 6LA
0171-937-8984
website: moebius.psy.ed.ac.uk/~spr/

Founded by scholars in 1882, the Society for Psychical Research is the oldest scientific organization devoted to paranormal studies. Its library in London, England, has one of the oldest and most comprehensive collections of literature on paranormal phenomena. The group currently conducts field studies on all such phenomena, including ESP, NDEs, OBEs, hauntings, and paranormal healings.

Suggestions for Further Reading

Books and Periodicals

Janet and Colin Bord, *The World of the Unexplained: An Illustrated Guide to the Paranormal.* London: Blandford, 1998. This book provides an overview of a wide variety of paranormal phenomena, including strange creatures, powers, and sightings. Although its text is brief, it has many photographs and illustrations.

Eileen Elias Freeman, *Touched by Angels: True Cases of Encounters of the Celestial Kind.* New York: Warner Books, 1993. This book offers stories and discussions of angel encounters from the perspective of a believer.

Karen Hastings, "Finding Religion: Apparitions Pique Interest in the Valley," *Dallas Morning News,* June 21, 1998. This article reports on various sightings of the Virgin Mary around the Dallas area, in such strange locations as a fried cornmeal biscuit and a car fender.

Hans Holzer, *The Directory of Psychics: How to Find, Evaluate, and Communicate with Professional Psychics and Mediums.* Chicago: Contemporary Books, 1995. This book offers information about psychic abilities, discusses the accuracy of psychics, and provides a listing of the most reputable professional psychics throughout the world, many of whom work with law enforcement agencies.

———, *Ghosts: True Encounters with the World Beyond.* New York: Black Dog and Leventhal Publishers, 1997. This large reference book is a compilation of stories related to encounters with ghosts.

Leon Jaroff, "Fighting Against Flimflam: James Randi," *Time,* June 13, 1988. This article profiles one of today's most famous skeptics, James Randi, a former magician and board member of the Skeptics Society.

Robin Mead, *Haunted Hotels: A Guide to American and Canadian Inns and Their Ghosts.* Nashville, TN: Rutledge Hill Press, 1995. This guidebook offers information regarding vacation places that have resident ghosts.

Melvin Morse with Paul Perry, *Transformed by the Light.* New York: Villard Books, 1992. This book discusses the ways in which people's lives have been transformed by near-death experiences.

Websites

The Faerie Encyclopedia (www.crosswinds.net/~rlehmann). This website offers a discussion of fairies that includes history, literature, and description information.

Paraweb (http://theparaweb.com). This website offers links to other sites related to a variety of paranormal phenomena, including aliens, UFOs, mysterious creatures and places, ghosts, psychics, NDEs, OBEs, reincarnation, and possible government conspiracies.

Sea Serpents and Lake Monsters (www.serve.com/shadows/serpent.htm). This website offers information about a variety of mysterious creatures sighted in bodies of water throughout the world.

Works Consulted

George O. Abell and Barry Singer, eds., *Science and the Paranormal: Probing the Existence of the Supernatural.* New York: Charles Scribner's Sons, 1981. Written by a professor of astronomy and a professor of psychology, respectively, this book offers a collection of articles on a variety of paranormal phenomena, many of them by leading skeptics.

David L. Bender and Bruno Leone, eds., *Paranormal Phenomena: Opposing Viewpoints.* San Diego: Greenhaven Press, 1997. This book for young adults offers articles related to a variety of paranormal issues, including NDEs, ESP, and UFOs.

Richard S. Broughton, *Parapsychology: The Controversial Science.* New York: Ballantine Books, 1991. The director of research at the Institute of Parapsychology, Broughton discusses psychic phenomena from the perspective of a believer, and offers scientific evidence to support his views.

Sylvia Brown and Antoinette May, *Adventures of a Psychic.* Carlsbad, CA: Hay House, 1998. This book is an autobiography of Sylvia Brown, a well-known clairvoyant.

Sophy Burnham, *A Book of Angels.* New York: Ballantine Books, 1990. This popular best-seller discusses encounters with angels from the perspective of a believer.

Paul Chambers, *Paranormal People.* London: Blandford, 1998. This book offers interesting information about people who have exhibited paranormal abilities such as precognition and telepathy.

Milbourne Christopher, *ESP, Seers, and Psychics: What the Occult Really Is.* New York: Crowell, 1979. Written by a magician, this book attempts to debunk psychic phenomena.

Jerome Clark, *Unexplained!* Detroit: Visible Ink, 1999. This book contains a large collection of stories related to a variety of paranormal phenomena, including UFOs, strange creatures, and the Cottingley fairy photographs.

Richard S. Cowles, "The Magic of Hypnosis: Is It Child's Play?" *Journal of Psychology,* vol. 132, July 1, 1998. This article offers an in-depth, scholarly discussion of hypnosis, providing new insights into an old phenomenon.

Alfred Douglas, *Extra-Sensory Powers: A Century of Psychical Research.* Woodstock, NY: Overlook Press, 1977. This book offers information about the early history of psychical research, including the work of the Society for Psychical Research in London.

Kenneth Frazier, ed., *Paranormal Borderlands of Science.* Buffalo, NY: Prometheus Books, 1981. This book is a collection of articles on various paranormal phenomena but is weighted toward those who approach these subjects with skepticism.

Nancy Gibbs, "Angels Among Us," *Time,* December 27, 1993. This article discusses the increased conviction among Americans that angels are real and offers opinions of both believers and skeptics.

Ted Harrison, *Stigmata: A Medieval Phenomenon in a Modern Age.* New York: St. Martin's Press, 1994. This book offers an in-depth discussion of the religious phenomenon known as stigmata and includes several interesting case studies from both the past and the present.

Roger Highfield, "The Hypnotic State Remains a Phenomenon That Divides the Experts," *Daily Telegraph,* August 15, 1998. This article discusses controversies related to the nature and use of hypnosis.

H. J. Irwin, *An Introduction to Parapsychology.* Jefferson, NC: McFarland, 1989. Irwin, who teaches parapsychology at the University of New England, offers a comprehensive overview of psychic phenomena.

David H. Lund, *Death and Consciousness.* Jefferson, NC: McFarland, 1985. This book provides a scholarly discussion of death and the human spirit, OBEs, NDEs, apparitions, hauntings, reincarnation, and religious faith.

Arthur Lyons and Marcello Truzzi, *The Blue Sense: Psychic Detectives and Crime.* New York: Mysterious Press, 1991. This book offers a thorough and interesting discussion of psychics who work with law enforcement agencies.

Susan Michaels, *Sightings: UFOs.* New York: Simon & Schuster, 1997. Based on a popular television show that presents supposedly true stories of paranormal phenomena, this book presents case studies related to UFO sightings.

Lance Morrow, "How to Believe in Miracles," *Time,* December 30, 1991. This article discusses the way that miracles are evaluated by religious leaders and laypeople.

Melvin Morse, with Paul Perry, *Closer to the Light: Learning from the Near-Death Experiences of Children.* New York: Villard Books, 1990. This book discusses NDEs using stories told by children who have experienced the phenomenon.

Michael Norman and Beth Scott, *Historic Haunted America.* New York: Tor, 1995. This book is a guide to haunted places throughout the United States that are visited by ghosts from America's history, as opposed to ghosts from modern times.

"The Power of Belief," hosted by John Stossel. Transcript of ABCNews Special, aired October 6, 1998. This hour-long television program attempts to debunk a variety of claims related to paranormal phenomena.

Champe Ransom, "Yes, Virginia, There Probably Is No Santa Claus," *Humanist,* vol. 57, November 21, 1997. Written by a skeptic, this article discusses the importance of accepting that certain beliefs, such as in Santa Claus, are not real.

Reader's Digest Association, *Mysteries of the Unexplained.* Pleasantville, NY: Reader's Digest Books, 1984. This book is a collection of stories related to paranormal phenomena, including prophecies, UFOs, miracles, and monsters.

J. B. Rhine and J. G. Pratt, *Parapsychology: Frontier Science of the Mind.* Springfield, IL: Charles C. Thomas, 1974. This scientific examination of psychic phenomena was written by two of the best-known researchers in the field.

Bill Roberts, "The Growing Mystery of Faith Healing," Gannet News Service, December 29, 1995. This article discusses Americans' belief in faith healing, offering the opinions of both believers and skeptics.

Pat Robertson, *Beyond Reason: How Miracles Can Change Your Life.* New York: William Morrow, 1985. Written by a Baptist preacher, this book argues that miracles are not only possible but a frequent occurrence.

David Van Biema, "Modern Miracles Have Strict Rules," *Time,* April 10, 1995. This article discusses the rules that the Catholic Church uses to establish whether a particular event is a true miracle.

Julie Wheelwright, "Friday Book: A Place for Belief in Miracles," *Independent,* April 2, 1999. This article discusses the healing miracles that have occurred at a shrine in Lourdes, France.

Diane Winston, "The Wonder of Miracles," *Dallas Morning News,* March 29, 1997. This article discusses the nature of miracles, offering the opinions of both believers and skeptics.

Index

Picture Credits

About the Author

Patricia D. Netzley received a bachelor's degree in English from the University of California at Los Angeles (UCLA). After graduation she worked as an editor at the UCLA Medical Center.

Netzley became a freelance writer in 1986 and is the author of several books for children and adults. She and her husband, Raymond, live in southern California with their children, Matthew, Sarah, and Jacob.